Awareness Fears
And Consequences

*An insight to understanding what
you can do to stay safe*

By

Alan Charlton

Photographs scanned by

New Breed
Po box 511
Dagenham
Essex RM9 5DN

Published by
New Breed Publishing

Printed and bound in Great Britain.

A CIP catalogue record for this book is available from the British Library

No part of this book may be reproduced by any means, nor transmitted, nor translated into machine language, without the written permission of the publisher.

ISBN 0 9538555 3 8

Printed in May 2002 (3rd edition)

New Breed Publishing
Po Box 511
Dagenham
Essex RM9 5DN
England

Our Web site www.newbreedbooks.co.uk

Our email address books@newbreed.worldonline.co.uk

Awareness Fears and Consequences
By Alan Charlton

Index

Dedication

Acknowledgements

Foreword

Introduction

Dedicated

To

Anyone who has felt their guts turn over with fear

And wishes they could do something

Acknowledgements

Thanks to:

Glenn Clark, Darrin Richardson Dave Turton and Kevin Fox
For all the phone calls and for sharing the high and low points of
being an Instructor.

Special thanks to Tony Falconer, Tim Clark and Sevim Necati
For all their help and assistance.

Jamie O'Keefe for all his help and support in putting this book
together.

Geoff Thompson for his permission to use the four D's and his
inspiration and support over the years, you're a lovely man Geoff
and I wish you and Sharon every happiness.

Peter Consterdine British Combat Association, for his support and
for giving me the confidence to set up the Self Protection
Association.

Steve Malone and Shaun Seymour for their friendship over the
years and for always being there.

To John Helliwell for making the cartoons come to life.

Master Ron, the first and still the best?

Mr Bill Hicks 16 Dec 1961 to 26 Feb 1994 A great comedian who
I never met But whose videos keep me laughing.

Last but not least my wife Caroline and my wonderful children
Aaron and Kate

Forward
By
Darrin Richardson B.Sc. CMS

I have known Alan Charlton for many years, I have trained with him taught and been taught by him. He is undoubtedly one of the jewels in the art of self-protection in the United Kingdom. In well over 28 years I have seen many instructors, not all can live up to their reputation. Alan however is one. He has trained with some very notable instructors learning his art and developing his own approach to the subject matter. He like many of his kind did not wake up one day an expert instructor, practitioner and author, His skills have developed over many years, and some two years ago he decided to write down many of the lessons he has learnt.

In today's society we live with the fact that we may at anytime be exposed to some sort of violence. This is not just a statement to scare you it is an every day occurrence; all you need to do is open your local paper or watch your local news. It's out there for all to see, just staring you right in the face.

Awareness, fears and Consequences are your Highway Code. We all read the Highway Code before we take our driving tests; we don't remember it all (well I don't) but we do remember the basics. It is those basics that help us drive round in relative safety.

It's the same with Self-protection; Alan Charlton has waded through all the unnecessary ideas and skills that have become the myth of the martial arts and self-defence. We the reader can quickly learn many valuable lessons from this book, without the pain of having first hand experience. This book is crammed full of information and humour and is a must for the library of those who take the subject seriously.

Darrin Richardson 4th Dan

AN INTRODUCTION

By Alan Charlton

Violence is something that does concern us all; from the bully in the play ground to the sometimes-insane violence found out side many public houses on a Saturday night. The brutal rape and murder statistics that we can see on the TV news or read about in the morning paper over breakfast just add to our fears. In no way do I put myself forward as being the best thing since sliced bread when it comes to understanding why some people are so brutal. I have found out the hard way that our fear of violence can make everyone of us feel that we are the weakest person on the planet. Feeling sick to the stomach with fear because of what might happen to us. Along with the entire contents of our personal invisible luggage we all carry full of, if buts and maybes. I felt that the answers to my questions as to how can I beat the bully in the play ground or stand up to the person who is about to kick off and beat the crap out of me, from training to find. The best fighting system to working the doors of clubs, pubs or looking after someone's private party, all to end this fear. It seemed to me then, that I was the only one who felt the fear of violence so bad. Knowledge is power, and for a long time I was looking in the wrong direction for the answers. And I was getting more impatient than a teenager looking to lose their virginity.

It is hard to put over to anyone how we feel inside, because for many of us that side of our self is deep within us. We harbour our loves and fears over years, maybe letting little bits of information come out from time to time. Sometimes this information can be turned against us so we may tend to hold more and more back, keeping our fears locked away. Maybe coming to terms with the facts years later or never admitting to them. But still lost in our fears that only we feel and only we have.

So I hope you will see yourself in some of the things I talk about in this book good and bad. This is a book on self-protection and no matter what your background it's just another piece of the jigsaw. Only you can put all the pieces together. Get information from anywhere you can, from books videos, courses and training will help. If you like, they are the straight edges of the jigsaw only time and a bit of hard work will fill in the rest of the picture.

In the beginning

In 1965 a beautiful baby boy was born, his parents loved him from the second he took his first breath. Over the years he grew strong and handsome, everyone who knew him wished they could be like him. He had it all. Unfortunately I was born in 1960 so I will start from there. I was born into a loving working class family with two older brothers. My Mum and Dad worked hard all their lives and gave me a good understanding of right and wrong. It was not always easy but the most important thing for me now looking back; was the love and up brining my parents gave me and I would not have changed a thing.

Like many children school was a real testing ground. Having to make new friends and the daily routine of uniform, books and lessons. Add the introduction of the playground bully. For most of us school is the first time we are introduced to conflict. Be it real, or the imaginary fears we have about the bigger boys in the next playground. For me Swimming and PE lessons were week-to-week battles, and sports day was an all out invasion. Because I've always had the type of figure that makes other people feel good about their own. Especially when they see the fat boy coming in last on the cross-country run, or displace more water in the swimming class than launch day in a shipyard. But it was always the same feeling I had inside, the name-calling and jokes hurt more than any physical attack I may have had at that time. But in 1974 I was hit by the reality of street violence. One summer's evening; some friends and I went to a party.

A friend of ours was helping out with a Disco and had invited us along. We were having a good time laughing and joking; the place was packed with college students and when you are only 14, college students seem like adults. At one point in the evening, we decided to go and get some air so we went out one of the fire exits and stood outside talking.

We had only been outside for about 10min when a group of lads came out and joined us on the fire escape.

Before I knew what was going on, one of the lads was shouting in my face.

"Was it you?" What the hell was going on, my friends and I were just standing here, now this man is shouting at me. I was bewildered, but I knew I had done nothing wrong so I thought he would stop and go away in a minute.

"No, Did what?" I said. Coming closer he shouted, *"It was fucking you."*

I was standing between steps on the fire escape one leg bent, the other straight with my back against the handrail. I had never been so scared, I was shaking all over and it was obvious to everyone. Trying to talk my way out I did my best. *"Please mate, I don't know what's going on, I've done nothing."*
He turned his head and said. *"Look what you fucking did, you pulled my fucking earring out."* CRACK, my legs were kicked from under me by one of his mates and the one who had been shouting punched me in the face as I went down. My arms instinctively rapped around my face. I could feel a pain in my side as I hit the steps. A mass of noise and confusion inside my head then they all started to kick me down the stairs. It was only about five or six steps, but it seemed to take forever. I couldn't do a dam thing to stop them. I just covered my head and kept screaming for them to stop, but they kept on going, right to the bottom step.

Less than a minute ago I had been laughing and joking with my friends and now I felt like I was in hell. Apart from begging them to stop I remember that my strongest thought was why? I had done nothing. When the kicking stopped, some people grabbed me and pulled me to my feet, "Are you ok mate? Lets get you cleaned up".

The next thing I remember was bending over and spiting blood into a toilet. Then trying to clean myself up with shaking hands and college paper towel (which is about as absorbent as cling film wrap) what a mess.

That beating I got in 1974 was a war in microcosm. It had all the key points that have been used by street attackers and even governments to attack their unsuspecting victims. They all start wars with dialogue, deception and then a pre-emptive attack. It's funny, looking back helps you to understand so much more. I was beaten badly by my attackers, but in a strange way I was also given the answers to how street attackers operate. In one painful lesson I was given all the answers, after 20 seconds of brutality all I had to do was understand the questions. But it would take me another 20 years before I could fully understand and would be willing to accept it.

For most of us, growing up is full of frustration, wonder, and sometimes pain. Some people's start in life is so hard it makes you wonder how the majority of them stay sane. For some they fight against all the odds and come out on top. The point I am trying to make is that from the moment we are born everything we experience shapes the way we interpret what is going on around us. An event or a place may make you feel safe, but for someone else it could be their worst nightmare. The experience I had in 1974, was my first real encounter with violence that was unprovoked and came at me unseen. In the playground it may have been bullying or name-calling, the bullies like to let you know they are coming it was all part of scaring the crap out of you. But when it comes at you out of the blue, the intimidation and the feeling of fear is so great you can remember it 20 years later.

This book is a personal view on self-protection, so what has the above got to do with it? Because people have different experiences, all of you reading this book will be taking the information on from a different standpoint. If you have been involved in a violent confrontation then this book will ring many bells. It will give you a guide to building your own personal protection system, to help you deal with the threat of violence or street confrontations. For a long time I kept looking for the answers to get rid of my fear of being attacked again. I tried many things all of which at the time I thought would make me into some type of fighting hero, I was so wrong.

I was given the wrong information for years, but like a good student I believed what I was told to be true. This system or that one, all telling me they would give me the answers in time. I could not see the wood for the trees. I was looking for physical techniques to help me feel safe and the more the merrier and it had to look good. I mean if I had to knock some attacker's teeth out I wanted to look good. How sad it all was. Violence is not a leaky pipe, or a broken Television. You will not have the time in the street to call and wait for the friendly repairman to get you out of trouble. I remember one time I was doing a leaflet drop around my local area advertising my club. I handed a lady one of my leaflets and she gave it back to me saying her husband was a Tae Kwon Do Instructor so she felt safe. When I gave her the leaflet, we were not on a busy street with lots of people walking about, we were on a quiet private road leading into some flats and she was on her own. You have to Do It Yourself. Most of us do not have the comfort of our own personal bodyguard with us 24 hours a day. Whenever violence enters your world you will be on your own, and you are the one who has to deal with it. A big problem is many martial arts Instructors do believe that what they are teaching has all the answers and will work in the street. The sport and fitness side of the arts is great. To train in a system for many years and perfect all of its fine movements takes dedication and hard work, and on a personal level is very rewarding. But, the fact remains that I know and have seen some great street fighters whose skills and knowledge to take care of themselves on the street is second to none, but have never entertained going to a martial arts class.

If you are looking for a book that teaches you lots of martial arts moves with a thousand and one combinations you have got the wrong book. Because of my training background I will talk about the martial arts from time to time in this book, and I do have a lot of respect for many systems and Instructors. But let's get things into perspective right now. If mainstream martial arts do not teach their students to understand that what works in the dojo (training hall) will not work for them in the street, then they are not being honest. It is a painful lesson for the student if they have to find out the hard way. That in a real situation, what they believed would work for them on the street is as effective as a chocolate fireguard

If you are training in one of the martial arts at the moment or you are about to join a club for the first time, this book will have something for you. We are all looking for the answers to our personal fears of street violence. And depending on our background and experience we are all at different stages of that journey. I believe that we all get to the truth in the end, it took me 20 years to find the answers, and the type of training that works for me.

The first question you have to ask is what are you looking for and what do you want from your training. Anyone that picks up a book on self-defence or goes to a local Karate class is looking for a comfort blanket. Something that they can just pull around themselves to feel safe. Most people are not looking to make it a life time journey of understanding. They want something that works now and does not make them feel too uncomfortable. This book will give you an insight into what areas you should be covering for protecting yourself in the street, how long and how far you wish to take your training is up to you. You can buy a book on how to drive a car or how to bake a cake, but at one time you have to get in and start the car or turn on the oven to see if the information works.

One of the most important reasons for writing this book is to help you save time. You do have to practise and think about your personal safety everyday and your safety is not a one off course or a one-book lesson. Understanding how you may be attacked and understanding by who, is the key to self protection. Most people feel it's being physically strong and knowing more kicking and punching combinations than your attacker. It's not, 90 percent is understanding and avoiding the physical confrontation. All the physical training you have done or about to do accounts for only 10 percent of what takes place in a real situation. So grab yourself a cup of coffee and the chocolate biscuits and let's work on that 90 percent.

Chapter 1

Simply Violence

What are you afraid of?

Being raped, glassed, killed, beaten, robbed or not having the bottle to fight back?
So what would be the worst thing that could happen to you? What would be your nightmare?

Every one of us will answer these questions differently and at different times in our lives our answer will change. You may well be worried about being attacked or maybe what you are going to have for dinner tonight or worried about your job. The list is endless and we do have the ability to change our priorities, some of us seem to do this on a daily basis. But if you get home and find that a loved one has been taken ill your priorities change quicker than your microwave takes to reheat your TV dinner. We should understand that every second of the day lays new opportunities and disappointments on our lap. It is up to us what we do about them. We may get it wrong at the time but when we wake up in the morning we get a second chance to make a difference.

Violence is something that can change people's perception on life. People's fears are real, but what most look for to help them with their fear of being attacked can let them down, and at the time of greatest danger. More than likely you will not be murdered in your bed or raped at knife point. But the fear of such violence is real and people are attacked daily. But if you put yourself forward for life insurance your health and age would come higher on the list than murder. So if you're a person who likes to bet then you could lay down pretty good odds.
People find themselves in confrontations every single second of the day. From falling out with the boss at work to screaming at someone over a parking space. There are thousands of people that we could quite easily react with in just one day in any busy city.

From travelling on the train to the hundreds of cars we drive or walk past. Out of the infinite combinations that can bring us together how can we see the small spark that explodes into violence?

The good news is, look at it like this. The majority of people around us feel the same. We may shout at each other from the car but most will not want to get out and stand face to face. You may be someone who can't stand any type of confrontation, and will move away at the first sign of trouble. And why not. It is something that we are brought up to understand. From a young age it's the bully or the victim and when all is said and done our basic instinct is to get away from danger. This is not a weakness but survival, basic and workable self defence. I mean you would not touch a hot iron twice to make sure it's hot would you? Unfortunately without fully understanding we can still end up feeling a victim at our own perceived weakness.

Your personal safety is something you should think about on a daily basis. With the right approach staying safe takes no more effort than it does to walk into a newsagent and buy a paper. But if your training or information does not reflect the lying, violent and brutal way real attacks work on the street you can kiss good bye to all your years of training. As for working in the street a snowball will last longer on a barbecue. Some of my ideas you may disagree with and that's fine with me, after all we all take on information from a different perspective. But people do tend to view a street fight as a cross between two talented fighters and an intricate battle plan. It's not. The battle plan for a street attacker is more like a vulture circling above you. When it does kick off it becomes a brutal pushing, kicking, scratching mess. When the victim falls to the floor the other vultures will arrive to take their bite out of the carcass.

Not all of us are keen to master the battle plans of a war, but we should and can deal with a single part of the whole. Most people can learn to ride a bike or drive a car within a short time, and well enough to get to the shops or just enjoy a ride in the park or a trip to the seaside.

But how many have the commitment to push and train themselves to ride or drive at a professional level? From a professional boxer to a top judo champion their level of training and commitment are light years away from what most of as are willing to go through. If we put as much effort into recognising dangerous situations as we do into preparing for a driving test we can stay safe. We learn and appreciate more as we go along just like after we pass the driving test. You now know how to physically move the car, but you now have more time to anticipate and react to the dangers and drive safely.

Why simply violence?

Because the physical act of protecting yourself against an attacker or the person beating the crap out of another person have the same underlining truth. It's physically easy to harm anybody. The doing and what you are prepared to do is the hard part. Someone's life can end in less time it takes to boil an egg, in a moment of madness a skull can be broken or a heart can be punctured. At what point would you feel its time to bite off your attackers nose or put your finger so far into their eye socket you feel their eye about to pop? Or does just the thought of doing something so brutal turn you off? To give you some idea of how long the fear can have hold of you, but the physical act itself only last a few seconds. One guy I had a run in with was going on for weeks. With many late nights talking to friends trying to find out what was going on. So many people were having a bad time because one person would not get their act together. I spent a day in a car waiting outside his flat for him to come home. If you ever done that, you will understand when I say even drinking two cans of Heineken will not refresh the parts of your body that have gone numb. After weeks of just trying to see this guy and talk over the problem he had with my friends it came to a head and we were face to face in his flat.

Now have you ever wondered how some people can be such a pratt, that even they can not miss the fact that when they open their mouth they are talking utter crap? Sorry to tell you all this but they are out there, and the truth is the last thing they are going to give you. Anyway back to the flat. It had got to a point that something was going to kick off. I did not want it to I just wanted this guy to do the right thing. I did not think the guy would get physical, but you can never be sure. Voices were raised along with all the lead up to an attack puffed out chests arms moving in all directions, as he turned into me. Crack his nose was spread over his face. Before I could bring my head back he was on the floor hands covering his face and sobbing like a baby. You would think with all the build up it would have ended up with a fight going for 14 rounds, with punches and kicks from all directions. No the physical bit was over in less than a second, one head butt had ended the whole thing. Being first stopped it, I was taken back by how the guy caved in. I was willing to take the fight on but that would have meant kicking a sobbing ball around the room and that's not me.

So in the great scheme of things the nuts and bolts of violence is simplicity. The mechanics of hitting is no greater than kicking a football or hammering a nail into a wall with a hammer. Its knowing the right time to get physical controlling and understanding the way you are feeling and if and when you have to, you kick off first. Be proactive not defensive because, if you are the one who gets hit first you are in a situation that many will not be able to fight back from. This is not a ring fight with a referee waiting to pull him off you, or a film set with the director calling cut and the stuntman comes in for the dangerous part.

We have to start with a basic outlook towards our personal safety right now. And that is proactive not defensive. To win at street level the answer is simple, If you can understand the ritual of an attack you can avoid most situations. But if you can't avoid, Hit first and Hit as Hard as You Can. Some of you may feel or have been told only to fight when the other person hits you first or you wait to be attacked. This is a dangerous way to view a confrontation, you will not have time to fight back. There are not many people who could come back after being hit first. Even the toughest and the best when confronted will always hit first and these guys if they had to could carrying on fighting long after most people would have given up. I feel you have to have a point at which you will fight, and be as hard and as brutal you can to win. No matter how small the confrontation they all have the potential to become life threatening. Your control should be on the situation before violence becomes your only way out. With most situations you do have time to avoid getting physical.

Training can give you confidence. Improving your punch or kick is important and many fighting systems spoil us with the number of techniques available. But getting them to work for you within the split second it takes for someone to attack you is hard. And most will never get close to understanding this within their normal class training. Many people find it hard to accept that from a small encounter an overwhelming situation can develop. Just the shock of finding oneself in the middle of a situation can make you unable or unwilling to do anything. Without the training to understand the situation, deciding what we should do becomes a grey area of indecision and at worst a poor physical response.

No Grey Area

A violent attack has no ifs, buts or maybes. Once the fists and feet are flying the attack is all over you like a rash. Many people feel the point at which you are committed to fighting is a grey area, it's not. Most situations can be avoided. If someone cuts you up in the car let it go, if you feel uncomfortable in a situation leave. If you stay in a situation that you are not happy with it's you who are making the outcome a grey area. It's more difficult when it's someone you know and a friendship is at stake. Because of my training and what I know works for me I can not kick off half way. In 99 times out of a 100 I will find a way out by backing off walking away saying anything at the time that will help me get away. One time I was confronted by an old friend. He was drunk. Something that happened a lot, not the confrontation but being drunk. But like a lot of old friendships you put up with a lot. But at this particular party he was being a right pain in the arse. Have you ever wondered where all the fun and laughter goes in a room when one person decides they have to be the centre of attention.

You could feel the happy atmosphere escaping from the room quicker than if someone had put on a Russ Abbot record of the same name. By hiding his drink and playing along with him, normally in time he would fall asleep in a chair and that would be the end of the matter. But this night was going to be longer than I thought, by one o'clock in the morning I was getting pissed off, yet another test to friendship. Clearing up some of the mess he had made I was taking some bits back to the kitchen when he blocked my path. I said to him *"come on mate it's late, everyone has gone. Get your head down and sleep it off"*.

This may have been the time he wanted to test himself or me, I'm not sure, but he was spoiling for a confrontation. "Who the fuck do you think you are telling me to go to bed" This may have been a drunken threat, but as he said it, he was moving towards me, if it had been anyone else I would have hammered him right there. I pushed him to one side not quite believing what was going on and made it into the kitchen. The rush of adrenalin hit me turning into anger as my feelings went into overdrive.

Like I said before violence is simple and can explode out of all proportion to what you feel is going on around you. I was standing in the kitchen shitting myself having to deal with all the emotion of the situation, and the feeling of what if it all gets out of hand. Recovering from the push he came to the doorway of the kitchen, I must have look very pissed off as I told him again to go and sleep it off. As I came out of the kitchen he was in my face again I could not bring myself to hit him so I pushed him against the wall. And told him that he was in no fit state to take me on and he still would not be if he was sober.

It sounds a bit corny now as I write it. But I was beating the crap out of him verbally with every word and threat I made to him and my hand pushing on his chest the words hit like punches. He had been fronting me up, me a friend who had put up with his crap for years and who had been there for him when he had been at rock bottom. I did not want it to come to blows and if it had been anyone else it would have, and been a lot easier to deal with and get over.

21

That was a big grey area for me because our friendship had been so close for many years, I mean you can't go round knocking out your friends. Maybe I should have ended the friendship sooner, not put up with it or only have seen him when he was sober. But very soon after that night our friendship was over, and as staying safe is a lot to do with moving away from trouble I will stay away. All of us can remember a person or a time we would have loved to have landed a right hook to their jaw or kicked them in the jewellery department for what they did or sent to us. We can play the idea over and over in our mind's eye for weeks or months afterwards, adding one more painful thing each time we think about it.

Can you imagine what a mess your life and the people around you would be in if everyone vented their anger by hitting out at everyone who upset them? I mean a security guard in a supermarket would be dealing with a fistfight over the frozen peas every two minutes. We all control want we do or say at some point. We have learnt to do this over a long time. As children we are set the ground rules as adult society sets the limits. All of which builds and strengthens our personal grey area. It's this that will stop us from fighting back at a time we are in danger. The fear of the outcome the panic of why, who and what do I do now fills your legs with jelly and your arms with lead shot. Your grey area has taken away your right to protect yourself. If the only outcome is a physical one then you have to switch on your attack like a light bulb hitting first and getting away as quickly as possible. Friends and family make it harder than dealing with someone who is a stranger. But we have years to get to understand friendships and we can always end them. Your attacker may seem weak he or she maybe physically smaller than you. You feel the situation is uncomfortable but you stay because you feel stronger than your attacker, you are adding a big grey area to the situation.

The Grey Clouds of Technique

With some simple training ideas (which you can add to any fighting system) you can be better prepared for the ugly truth. To learn over many years the fine details of any fighting system is rewarding on a personal level but to transfer the same ideas as workable off the mats is dangerous. A student who is taught if someone grabs you do this, grab the attacker's wrist. Twist this way and that way pull them to the ground then lock and control the arm. Or you maybe grab from behind just reach over with your hand and grab their little finger and pull it back, turn under and away from them and strike at the pressure points in their forearm. I'm sure many of you like me have seen or trained with this type of outlook towards dealing with an attacker. Now what do you make of this one?

Someone is right in your face telling you that you're the wanker, who just looked at his girlfriend. Poking his finger in your chest and screaming in your face, with breath so bad a pig would brush his teeth to get rid of it. Before you can reply he grabs the back of your neck and hits you in the face with a half empty beer glass. As I said you may not agree with my ideas and the beer glass may be extreme, but the point I'm making is that many ideas put forward to deal with an attacker fall apart when your training partner just turns up the pressure. Your personal grey area when it comes to violence can only be controlled when you have the belief in yourself and that your techniques work under pressure. It is possible to train for the reality of street combat and in a safe manner. As long as you understand that however uncomfortable you may feel in your training it can only show you part of the picture. If you take away the comfortable part of your training and put yourself under pressure it can only improve your understanding of yourself and what you can make work under pressure.

Once a fight kicks off your ability to control it is almost impossible. It is an uncontrollable mess. Remember that unlike any competition it is rare to be dealing with just one person. Dealing with the situation beforehand or taking control in the first few seconds is where most of us will be able to do something to get away and home safely. If you can feel the heat and smell the smoke would you wait for the fire alarm to ring before you got out? Of course not. That isn't a grey area. You would be on your toes to safety because your life is on the line. The media and the fire services tell us to fit fire alarms and make plans for an escape route to get out of the building as quickly as possible. Never go back into the building to try and save valuables or even a copy of your favourite book by Jamie O'Keefe.

It is not a weakness to back down or walk away from a situation that is dangerous. If the first thing you hear is the alarm ringing in your office you may joke about it in the car park if it was a false alarm. But thankful to be outside if the building was on fire. But if say a locked door was blocking your escape route, you would pick up the fire axe and break it down, you would not be worried about what your boss would say about the broken door, you just have to get out. The black and white of violence is something to which you do have a say, when you decide to fight back it must be for something more than a spilt drink or someone jumping the queue, you have to set the limit.

Things piss me off every day. Many times I have walked away from situations that afterwards fill me with such anger and frustration, I would love to have lash out and its hard not to. I don't work the doors of nightclubs anymore. No one is paying me to stand there and take the abuse. Because I train not to hold back any part of my physical response to what I consider dangerous situations, and train with people who will and can put me under pressure and my physical limits. This goes a long way to help me control the grey area and know at what point I am willing to kick off.

When do I fight?

It would be great if we had some type of override fight mechanism inside us that automatically switched in whenever danger came knocking. Something that would turn on the gas and accelerate us into action rather than the feeling of having both feet jammed on the brakes. Before you make the decision to fight you have to understand that it is a choice that must be made before any situation develops. I do not mean you walk down the street half-cocked just waiting for someone to say the wrong thing.

There are enough of these types of people walking around any city on a Friday or Saturday night. Remember you can see most situations develop. If it feels uncomfortable get out of the club or pub or move to a different part of the venue. If you feel the £10.00 entrance fee gives you the right to stand your ground in the club no matter what, then good luck. If you think about all the times you have been out for a drink, meal, club, cinema or just out shopping in one year it runs into hundreds. Now how many times have you been attacked once, twice, never? So on the rare occasion you have to leave a £20.00 round of drinks or an entrance fee what's the problem.

I'm sure most of you would agree that a professional Bodyguard or nightclub doorman are people who are very capable of physically looking after themselves. But the majority of their training is used to spot potential problems. The bodyguard may take his VIP into the back entrance of a hotel to avoid the crowds. The doorman may tell someone they can't come into the club, because the person may be drunk or the doorman feels that this person could be a problem. This is using proactive judgement; they are taking away the chances for something developing that could be a problem.

When you feel under threat of being physically attacked this is the time to act. You don't wait for the person to hit or grab you, trying to work your way out of this, is a nightmare. The harsh reality is that although it is essential to train realistically. Without the ability to see situations develop ('being aware') the likelihood is that a situation will deteriorate to such a degree, that even the most accomplished fighter will struggle to survive or won't know what happened until it's all over. The answer to when do I fight is when you feel you have no choice. This is not a cop out on my part. Only you know when you feel something is worth fighting for.

How do I know it will work?
What? How many people you can knockdown with just one punch or just to keep your bottle under pressure and be able to walk away from a situation and keep your ego in your pocket. Both are hard, very hard to answer.

But I'm sure many of you reading this have had to walk away from confrontation and have had to deal with the feeling of being weak and backing down. If so you should not feel bad about it. To some degree you must have had control of the situation to get away without being physically attacked. Ok so you may feel bad about yourself because your ego took a beating but you are showing great strength in keeping that control.

If a situation does get physical you need techniques that can work for you under pressure. You don't need lots of them just one or two ideas that work for you. But you have to believe in them one hundred percent and the only way is for you to try them out under pressure. Most people are not willing to do this type of training but some form of pressure test is the only way you will know what works. You don't have to jump in with both feet, just start adding a bit at a time. Lets say you train hitting a shield or focus mitt try hitting when they are moving or when the person holding them runs at you. As you build up the pressure you cut down on the number of different techniques you use. In the end you may be left with just a right hook and a back fist but if you can make them hit the target hard every time you have something that works for you.

To work in the street it has to be simple. There are, of course, those who would disagree and think they could quite easily perform complex techniques under pressure. Its ok for them to live in a fantasy world, but to pass on their ideas about what they think will work on the street or in a pub car park is dangerous.

Let's look at this old favourite; wait to be attacked first. If this is your first rule for when to fight make sure your second is only fight back when you are within easy reach of a Hospital. If you feel you can only understand an attack is taking place when someone is throwing a punch at you, you have been very lucky. In all the years I have been training I have worked with and seen some great people very capable of looking after themselves. And as I said before I could count on one hand the ones that could still fight back after taking a punch to the jaw. In no way would they be happy about it they would always prefer to take the lead.

You are the one who has to say to yourself, *"Would this work for me in the street? What am I looking for, to protect myself or enjoy learning and practising an art form"?* You are the one who has to believe and know it will work. Your emphasis should be firmly on awareness and avoidance measures. It's no good saying I would do this or that if my life depended on it. If you have never put yourself under the mental pressure and the physical frustrations of training for a real encounter, what you think and what you do are two different things.

We are all different, and every one of us has a different level at which we will kick off. And that personal level will also change depending on the type of day we have had. Most of us have encountered some form of rage, be it in a car or standing in a queue. Luckily for most of us we can work through this stress and get through the day. But it does stay within us and can explode at anytime and when it does the results can be deadly, we could find ourselves at war for little more than a car parking space.

CHAPTER 2

Awareness

For any one to understand the routine way in which we often use the word violence. It has to be said that many of us have been desensitised to the brutality of what is for many a single word. And one word cannot justify the crippling way it ends many good people's lives.

Awareness

"Yes your attacker may be strong, Yes he could be bigger and taller than you, but you can win, no one should be a victim, you can be harder and stronger than you think."

Violent attacks, and the fear of violence is something that every one of us at one time or another will feel, or be involved with. The attacker today appears to be getting more and more extreme in his or her attacks be it physical or verbal. It may be hard for us to understand how someone can smash a beer glass into someone's face, just because they pushed by him and spilled his drink. How someone after demanding money can then stab the person they have just robed in the chest with a screwdriver, and leave them dying on the pavement, for just a few pounds is nightmarish to think about.

You may believe it only happens in books or on television, but it does happen on the street and at times when most of us feel safe. We may not like to think about the examples of the screwdriver or someone smashing a beer glass into someone's face. But it happens, and on regular enough bases to be a real problem. We have to accept the fact that there are people who do commit brutal acts of violence. Without any fear of the damage they will do to their victim, or have any concern for any legal consequences of their actions. For most of us this type of attacker is hard to understand, to us it may be just a ten-pound note or a cheap wristwatch.

But for the person robbing you it could be the money he needs to get that next drink or drugs fix which for a few hours will stop him feeling the pain of withdrawal. I am not asking you to feel sorry for your attacker nor am I making excuses for him. But one thing that is important to understand, is the fact you cannot equate your sense of moral justice to your attacker. They are working on a completely different set of rules.

It doesn't matter if you are young or old, male or female at some point you will be involved in some form of confrontation. Luckily for the majority of us it will not be a shooting or a stabbing. It may be just a verbal exchange over a parking place or someone jumping the queue at your local supermarket. But the anxiety you will feel in those few seconds of confrontation can have a big effect on you. The unforgettable feeling of stress you get inside can last for a long time. Understanding how situations can develop, and recognising the key danger signs before the verbal confrontation becomes a physical attack, is frequently over looked by too many groups and so-called self-defence instructors. If you add some of the impractical techniques these people then try and put across as workable, it's like sending someone into a minefield and telling them if they step on a mine, just jump out of the way of the blast and rollover into a ball. Surely it must be a better approach to look and see the warning sign saying, "Beware minefield" and then taking a different path? Or if you find yourself in the middle of a situation understand how you can disarm the danger or control the explosion.

Awareness, fears and consequence, understanding and dealing with these 3 main points are the most important parts to self-protection. As I said in the introduction only 10 percent is using physical techniques and I will cover the punching and kicking part later in the book. Please don't start flicking to the back of the book for the violent kicking people in the teeth bits.
Without understanding what is going to be happening to you in that 90 percent, you are more likely to wet your pants than throw a punch. Your real fears are in the front of this book. If you don't get

to grips with them now it may take a kicking and 20 years to understand.

We can and will work on that important physical bit later but first grab another cup of coffee and read on, we can play at being Rambo later.

"If you are not aware of the danger all the physical training and preparation in the world will not help you."

I feel the biggest part of staying safe on the street or anywhere is looking at what is going on around you. Being aware of the people around you or what type of place or area you are in. When you add the fact that most victims of an attack say they did not see their attacker or say he came out of nowhere and just hit me. The point should be made for the majority of street attacks the victim did have time to act. But for whatever reason they ignored the signs or could not understand the threat at the time. For me standing on

"Its this way kids, come on"
If you are not aware of your surroundings you could be in big trouble

that fire escape as soon as the lad's came out onto the fire escape I should have had all my alarm bells ringing. I did not, so I was a victim. I do not want to go into the right or wrongs of why someone enjoys beating the crap out of someone they have never met. Or attacks and rapes a woman just because she happened to be walking along a particular street.

This type of crime goes on everyday and greater minds than mine have not come up with the answers. We don't have to like the idea, but we have to accept that some people are prepared to commit unbelievable acts of violence.

If you believe that you should have the right to walk down any street or go into any pub or club at any time, without the threat of being attacked, I would like to agree with you.

It would be great to live in a world like that. But we live on this planet. Where some of its so-called higher species will attack members of their own species for the slightest reason. So lets not get too bogged down with the rights and wrongs and deal with how to see the problems and deal with them. The good news is that if you get the awareness right the chances of being involved in a physical confrontation are greatly reduced. You just have to accept that sometimes it's better to walk away than to stay because your ego is telling you to.

We are happy to follow the rules if we are driving a car around town. If the traffic lights turn red we stop and wait. We know if we ignore the lights and drive across there is a very good chance that we will be involved in an accident. We are happy not to take a chance, and wait for the lights to change. With a green light we know that it's safer to drive on. So driving is using basic awareness skills. If we drove around without being aware or following the basic rules of the road, we would run into trouble sooner rather than later.

If we take note of our feelings and what is going on around us we can see trouble coming from a long way off. If we ignore them, an unseen attack is deadly and a very hard position to win from. Like a rabbit that hops into the middle of the road he is out of his normal environment and vulnerable, normally if he heard a twig crack he would be off. But in the middle of the road he is unaware of the danger and finds himself staring into the headlights of an on coming car. If only he would hop a foot or two one way or another he would be safe and could get home in time for tea and carrot cake with his friend Benjamin. But he can't he is fixed to the spot by the car headlights, he can hear the car coming but cannot move or do anything about it. Hopping is something he can do at any time and without thinking about it. But as the lights of the car come nearer and nearer the simple act of hopping seems impossible. Shaking with fear, the car is almost upon him, he knows he should get out of the way; he tries to one last time, BANG! Too late, in the road lies another victim.

Being aware is accepting that you are always in unfamiliar surroundings, and seeing the car could be a threat before the headlights fix you to the spot. It's the same as you not being aware of the person coming towards you, and when he suddenly starts shouting in your face you will be frozen to the spot, and an easy victim. For an attack to take place you need 3 things: a victim, an aggressor and an opportunity. If you take away any one of the 3 the attack or crime cannot take place. You may or may not see yourself as a victim; most people don't until they are involved in a crime or confrontation. But only you can take control of your state of awareness, remember take away one of the 3 and it can't happen. And out of the 3 things you are the easiest one to control and stop the 3 elements of an attack coming together.

You could think of it like this, when you leave your home to go out to the shops or go to work you secure your home. Closing the windows and shutting the door behind you. You are aware of the dangers of leaving your doors and windows open because you are aware of the possible danger of someone breaking in and taking your property. Now if you have never had someone break into your home and you live in an area where the incidents of burglary are low, your awareness of the danger may drop off. Because you are only popping down to the local shops for some milk, you may leave the small window in the bathroom open. Being so small who could fit through that window. On leaving you may not lock the door just leaving the latch lock on. You are making your property an easier target/victim and giving someone a better opportunity to break in, all you need now is the burglar to be in your area and the 3 elements can come together.

It is a devastating feeling to find that someone has come into your home marched around your personal space and taken your private things. It turned out to be an expensive pint of milk, but a lesson learnt. You have no wish to go through the experience again so you make sure to lock up before you go out. Adding extra locks to the windows and doors and may be an alarm. You are making your home more secure by giving the burglar less time to get in and out of your property, making your home a harder target and taking away the opportunity.

Now it is not possible to rule out never having your home broken into again. It depends on how much the burglar wants what is inside your home. If you had Vincent Van Gogh's painting of sunflowers hanging in your kitchen a determined burglar would break in. You could be as high Tec as you like with your security arrangements if the prize is big enough some people will test every safe guard you make.

We must be responsible for taking control of how we look and put ourselves forward to others. If it is obvious that you are carrying something very valuable then the higher the chance of someone willing to take it from you. If you walked round any shopping centre with your wallet hanging out of your back pocket or your handbag open someone will very likely take a dip. I hope you are thinking to yourself that this is obvious. That's right and the very point I'm trying to make is that we all have a basic idea of awareness, but we don't always believe its going to happen to us. It can be quite a shock when you find yourself in a position where you feel you are in danger of something going to happen.

Many years ago my wife and I took part of our honeymoon in New York City, a place we had always wanted to see. When we arrived in New York I must admit the figures for violent crime and the amount of firearms in the city I had read about did flash through my mind. Working and living in London for most of my life gave me a good sense for being streetwise. But the gun thing puts it on a higher level. The excitement of being in Manhattan riding in yellow cabs seeing the sights and eating some of the best steaks I've ever had put the gun thing further to the back of my mind. For part of our stay we had booked a flight on a helicopter, which would fly us around Manhattan Island. We were both very excited about the flight not only for the view but also the idea of being in a helicopter, a first for both of us. On the day of the trip we made sure we were there on time. In fact we walked the route in half the time we had worked out from the street map the night before. The flight and the views over the Island were fantastic. If you ignore the rest of the information in this book please take this one piece of advice: if you ever get the chance to ride in a helicopter take it, great fun.

The flight was over too quickly. Still buzzing from the trip and my amazement at the fact the rotors on the helicopter were so powerful they could even lift me up-diddly-up-up. We had been walking back to our hotel but had not been paying attention to the direction we had started walking. New York is a great city and like all cities of the world has areas that you would be better off not visiting. The streets are laid out as a grid. It's easy to find your way around, but if your mind is elsewhere you can soon find yourself in trouble. We had been told about this particular street and not to walk down it, cross it at the major junctions but never walk-down it. Yes, you guessed it, we found ourselves walking down the street we had been told not to go down. We did not see the street number. We just had this feeling of being very uncomfortable with our surroundings. As soon as we made a comment about our surroundings to each other everything hit our senses. How run down the area looked, some of the names of the clubs and Bars and the smell of grass (not the type you cut on a Sunday afternoon) coming from a group of people in front of us.

We made a beeline for the next junction and as soon as we turned the corner the atmosphere changed and I'm not joking, it was that quick. We were not attacked, robbed or physically threatened in anyway but the fear was real. We had switched off to our surroundings so much that when we did tune into the danger it scared us. If someone had taken advantage of the two Londoners walking around I don't think I would have been able to do a dam thing about it. We had switched off to our surrounding and become unaware of any dangers that where around us, we had easy target and victim written all over us.

White the colour of Violence

"You can drive the safest car in the world, but with your eyes closed you will still drive over the cliff."

The fear of a violent attack can be greater then the reality. We all tend to think about the worst case scenario. From being raped by a hooded knife-wielding maniac, attacked by an armed gang. Yes, these types of violent attacks do happen and it is a concern, but they are rare. For the majority of us they are something that we are more likely to read about in the newspaper or see on the television screen than have first hand experience of. But all of us at one time will be involved with a confrontation in one form or another. No matter how small the incident the effect it can have upon you can be devastating.

From the verbal attack by another car driver, someone pushing in front of you at the bus stop or the person who eats crisps behind you in the cinema? Who having been satisfied with the explosions and people being shot to pieces in the film. His brain cells cannot cope with complex dialogue and, god forbid a plot. So his mouth opens to the size of a dustcart as he cascades crisps from a great height in total ignorance of all around him. We have all at one time felt the aggression build up inside us, and wished we could grow to the size of Arnold Schwarzenegger and put the person in the nearest dustbin. For many of us this is the type of situation that, if we let it could quickly escalate into a violent exchange. What would you do if this person were sitting behind you in the cinema? Would you move to another seat? Ask them to show some manners and keep the noise down or wait for him to finish the packet of crisps?

Studies have shown that communication consists of body language, voice tonality and words; this in itself may not seem remarkable. But when you realise that body language accounts for 55%, voice tonality 38% and words 7% of communication you may understand what an important role body language has in self protection. Most muggers will have already decided who their victim is before any words are exchanged. So therefore it follows that a person's body language is the deciding factor when a mugger looks for a victim. The size, shape, colour or age of their intended victim is not always a high priority. The fact that someone is unaware of the danger, is the person/victim they are looking for and what makes their job a lot easier. Awareness and body language are inter-related. Your body language will broadcast for all to see your state of awareness, being aware will give you time to react to any situation.

It's up to you to take the first and most important step in protecting yourself, getting switched on.

Question. If you went into a restaurant and found rats running over the tabletops would you be happy to eat there? If a good friend had told you he had been sick for week after eating there, would you have made the trip in the first place? If you answered NO to the questions, then you have used judgement and information to avoid a situation, which could have been damaging to your health. If you answered YES, you obviously like taking risks and have a cast-iron stomach or a good supply of toilet paper. So we can all make judgements about which would be the right thing to do, and with the right information we have time to make a choice. So what we need is a way to help us see the possible dangers in time. Seeing a rat in a restaurant triggers a response of information built up over years of relating rats with dirt and disease. We don't have to see the state of the kitchen to know that we should try a different restaurant. Just seeing the rat would be enough information to get us to move on.

We all have a personal built in safety radar. The problem is we tend to disregard the warning ping until the danger is much greater and therefore much harder to deal with. We need away of seeing the danger in stages, say by degrees of threat, a visible warning like traffic lights. Colour coding your levels of awareness as you walk down the street is just one way you can get, and keep switched on. Being switched on to your surroundings will change your body language and will automatically broadcast that you are aware and not an easy target. So what is colour coding? It's a way of keeping control and automatically reacting to different situations. Like driving a car if you turned a corner and the traffic lights were amber. Because you know the sequence of the lights you know you have time to stop the car. Working the colours of awareness is easy. It can be broken down into 4 easy steps: White, Yellow, Orange and Red each colour indicating your level of awareness.

White-Switched Off. White is the danger colour and is the colour of violence. At this level of awareness you are disregarding the warning pings of your radar. White is the colour most people use going about their daily lives or who find themselves lost in New York. In white you are broadcasting the fact to anyone who is looking out for the signs that you are a victim. You may as well be at home asleep with all your doors and windows open with a sign over the front door saying *"come in and help yourself."*

Yellow-Switched ON. This is the level of awareness we should be in at all times. As you walk down the street or into a shop, club or get into a train, make a mental note of the people around you. Before you stop reading this book because you think this guy is a nutter, getting people to feel paranoid about walking down the street. You are wrong. Being aware of your surrounding is common sense. You drive your car in code yellow, are the lights green or red? Minor, signal, manoeuvre etc. So being in code yellow is no more than looking and making a mental note of who or what is around you. At this level you are making mental judgements as to the people and places around you. So if someone pushes past you, if you are switched on to the fact that this is the second time they pushed by you, they may look OK but what are they up to. You can move away from that area of the street, club or train station and have automatically shown your level of awareness.

Orange- Avoidance. Most attacks happen when the victim is in code white (switched off). If you are switched on (code yellow) you will see most situations develop. If you are aware, you will see the person standing at the end of the street if you do not like the look of him, cross the road. If you walked into a pub and the floor was covered with blood and bodies were hanging from the fake oldie world barn ceiling you would leave. Or if driving your car and ahead of you the traffic lights turned red you would stop. So not being aware would be like driving down the motorway with your eyes closed. In code orange you are taking action to get away from a situation that you feel to be a danger. If you stay in a place that you feel uncomfortable with, you are putting yourself in danger and giving yourself fewer chances to get away safely.

Red- Fight or Flight. After all your efforts of avoidance and the unlikely event that the person moves into attack or just gets too close. This is the time to take action, pre-empt the attack by getting away or striking first then getting away as fast as you can. Fighting back is the last course of action, not because I think it's wrong to hit people who maybe about to hit me. Rather, if I get the awareness right I can be away before the last course of action is the only one left to me. If the attack has got to the point that the person has physically got hold of you, the time for talking is over. They have already picked you out as a victim. If the attacker pushes you and runs off with your bag or case, let it go. Going after the attacker will only put you in more danger. But if you are locked in a situation and you feel that the person is about to attack you, you have to be prepared to fight. Because if you truly believe that the person is going to attack you, this is the only thing that should push you into fighting. But once the decision is made make it hard fast and be first. If you wait for the physical attack it will be too late and you will be involved in a real blood and snot fight and unless you train for this it will be hard to get away.

The Crime Triangle

VICTIM

CRIMINAL

For any crime to take place you need

OPPORTUNITY

COLOUR CODING

An American Firearms specialist first introduced this system. It is equally effective in self protection. The system allows us to categorise situations with colours and associate a response to these colours; this reduces thinking time saving vital seconds.

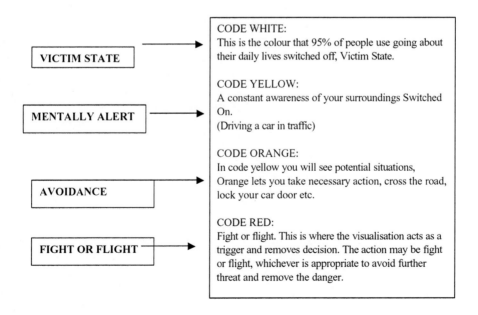

VICTIM STATE

MENTALLY ALERT

AVOIDANCE

FIGHT OR FLIGHT

CODE WHITE:
This is the colour that 95% of people use going about their daily lives switched off, Victim State.

CODE YELLOW:
A constant awareness of your surroundings Switched On.
(Driving a car in traffic)

CODE ORANGE:
In code yellow you will see potential situations, Orange lets you take necessary action, cross the road, lock your car door etc.

CODE RED:
Fight or flight. This is where the visualisation acts as a trigger and removes decision. The action may be fight or flight, whichever is appropriate to avoid further threat and remove the danger.

Awareness, or Just Paranoid?

If you are comfortable walking down the street or having a drink in a local pub then that's great, enjoy the walk and the drink. The grim reaper is not standing on every street corner, or about to walk into every pub. That's being paranoid. Being aware is the key. But what if on that walk to the local pub, you see a man showing a small child the finer points of hitting a ball with a baseball bat. Your mind puts this together as father and son bonding, sunshine and birds singing, a happy family scene. But as you leave the pub later that night, you see a man walking towards you with a baseball bat. The image is no longer a happy family scene, this time the feeling is very uncomfortable. The hairs on the back of your neck are sending you alarm signals. Would you cross the road to get out of his way, or ask him if was going to late night baseball practise?

If all situations on the street were as easy to see we would have no problems going about our day to day lives. The attacker on the street today will not be so obvious. He will pick out a victim, and strike when you are off guard, taking you by surprise. From walking up to you smiling and saying, "Excuse me mate, do you know the way?" BANG! Before the question is finished you have been hit and on your way down. It is common for an attacker to ask a question or engage his victim in conversation before attacking. We are taken off guard and thinking about the question, we cut out the information that is telling us that this could be a dangerous situation. Because all of us are bomb barred with information every second, minute and day of our lives. To keep control we can and do block out, a lot of this information.

Just take the simple act of leaving your house in the morning and getting into your car so you can get into work. The amount of information we have to get though to do all the physical acts is one thing, getting dressed, making breakfast etc. If you then add just some of the things we are hit with from outside this can stop us in our tracks and we have to file that information before we can continue. You could be in the middle of shaving, comparing the smoother cutting edge of your new razor over the old one.

Looking at yourself in the minor you squint at your refection, that's better 5 years younger? When over the radio comes the traffic report, the radio has been on all the time. But you have been listening to it on a sub-conscious level. But now your brain has triggered a response, this is important all your attention goes to the radio. *"The M1 motorway has a 5mile tail back at junction 3 south bound."* Big smile of relief, that's ok you are north bound today. You switch the radio back to sub-conscious listening and get on with the job of making your self look more human?

So we are making conscious and sub-conscious judgements all the time. Like the radio we need to have a way of switching onto the dangers, if you like tuning into the danger signals. Giving us personal radar that can pick out potentially dangerous situations before its too late. If you can see it or know it's there, you can do something about it. We don't have to learn any strange or mystical skills, we have them already and we use them all the time, we just have to switch it on and use it. Again most attacks are not out of the blue. You do have time to see and make judgements about how you wish to act or the action to take. The fight or physical bit of an attack is a very small part of the picture. Finding away to give yourself an early warning system that can cut out the day-to-day bits, but can switch on in time and give you an easy to follow plan.

You have to deal with the situation before it's in your face, or you are going to have to work very hard at get away from it, if at all. Understanding and giving yourself a set of levels of danger will get you working and thinking about your safety and possible dangers in advance. Staying switched on is the important part in protecting yourself and staying out of any street confrontation. Most victims of street crime think the person came from nowhere and just attacked them. The chances are that the attacker had been observing them for sometime and may have bumped into them to check their state of awareness many times. The street attacker will always take the easy option and most will move away if they feel that you are switched on. More to the point, the potential attacker will see that you are aware from a distance and may not even come close to you. So how can we prepare for this? First anyone who is in your personal space is a threat. No I'm not being paranoid just because someone moves into my personal space. It's because the person is a stranger, and as they are asking me a question they are still moving into my space.

Look at it this way, the last time you asked someone a question on the street that you did not know, I bet as you asked the question you spoke in a softer voice and stood some distance from them and waited for their reply. Why do we do this? From the day we are born we learn the social skills of our society, and being too close when asking a question, or just in polite conversation is one of them. Remember their body language will give you more information than what they are saying to you. The social learning we get in our early years is deep rooted. As adults we can find ourselves working hard to override the feeling just because we do not wish to appear rude. So if someone is too close you must make the first move. You could step back, giving distance to make the point that you feel they are too close. At this point if it was something more than a person asking a question, they would see you were aware. Without the element of surprise they could back off. If they don't, the fact that you have reacted in a positive way means you cannot be taken by surprise. So what colour code would someone asking you the time in the street trigger? Yellow, how many people, Orange where and how are they standing. If you blindly look at your watch you are open to attack. I'm not saying you drop kick the person or knee him in the nuts because he wanted to know the time. If his body language and distance feel comfortable tell him the time. But if he moves in close you move up your colour code and your threat assessment. Don't put up with feeling uncomfortable. Your subconscious is telling you something is wrong, listen to it.

This may seem a lot to take in. *"Too bloody right mate, thinking about colours on my way home from work. Who, what and how many people around me? Christ, if I did all that I would be late for my train and not get home in time for EastEnders"*. Again we all take on information at different rates and what many people believe to be the answer to protecting themselves must be a physical one. It's not in a short time you can develop a keen sense when it comes to how you view people on the street. In a real situation you will be limited by the surprise of an attack and in many cases any combat or self defence training you have done will fall apart. Keeping aware at all times and getting to understand your feelings of how dangerous a situation feels to you at the time. This is more important than learning 50 ways to get out of someone grabbing your wrist.

Most situations will not end up with a violent outcome, most will fade-away once the threat has passed.

I was out with a friend one time and we had to cross a busy road junction in London, with safety in mind we used the subway. As we were walking along the tunnel about half way, 3 guys entered the subway at the far end and were walking towards us. Still walking and talking to my friend I moved away from the tunnel wall so I was on the outside of my friend. This stopped our conversation for a second but we were still moving forward and I had time to take a quick look behind me. As we got close to the 3 guys we all had to move a bit so we could pass each other, one of them looked at me and I replied with a little smile and an "Alright" No one stopped we all kept walking. I could hear them walking away from me, but when my friend and I got to the foot of the stairs of the subway I turned just to make sure they had gone. Again the guys did not threaten us nor did they seem intimidating I was just aware of them.

This level of awareness is so common place that if it had not been for my friends comments about my conduct I would have forgotten about it by now. I think my friend was concerned for me. In fact he feels that, I seem to react may be just a little bit too much. Justifying my actions to my friend was to make me seem even more intense. I had seen the guys as they entered the subway my friend could only remember me moving to one side. I was assessing the threat I said. What threat? The guys looked ok to me, my friend said. Yes they did, but tell me what does an attacker look like? Ok, let's break it down. One, I don't know who or what the guys were doing walking down the subway. *"More than likely to cross the busy junction the same as us"*, my friend said. Yes 99times out of a 100 that's true. Because I had seen them as they entered the subway and also that no one else was behind us, this helped me keep assessing the threat levels. By moving out from the wall I could line up my attack on the one of the three I was going to hit first if it had become a problem. *"Christ Alan, don't you think that's just a bit paranoid, if you walk around thinking that every one you see is going to be a problem you are going to get ulcers"*. Said my, by now very concerned friend.

No you're seeing it as something that brings on a high stress level it's not. As long as the threat is at a low level and stays at that level, that only needs me to move from where I'm sitting or take an exit out of the way of trouble, no more stress. When you make awareness part of your day-to-day life the doing becomes automatic. It would be much more stressful to be involved in violent confrontation. The fact is that we can and do use threat assessment all the time. From crossing the road to driving a car, all acts that take judgement and second to second assessment of danger or if you like levels of threat.

If I see a situation as a threat and that an attack is about to take place. I'm in a better position if I know what my next action is going to be. Like someone driving a car keeping an eye out for other road users, the driving part is being done automatically. In the same way if a child ran out in front of the car the driver's reaction would be to hit the brake as hard as they could. Because the driver has been prepared for the possible dangers he may come across when driving. As soon as he sees the child and the danger he has a physical reaction. He pushes down on the brake pedal. If the driver was driving down an unfamiliar road he could be alerted to the danger by road signs for crossing, school or speed restrictions. This will not have you hitting hard on the brake pedal but preparing you for possible danger, this goes on mile after mile for as long as you are driving. Would you consider yourself paranoid when you are driving? Or would you feel you are making a basic threat assessment and using good driving skills?

44

Yes there are times when with all the best will in the world we are taken off guard, when out of blue something takes you by surprise. From someone bumping into you in the high street and taking the wallet from your top pocket or someone jumping a red light at a junction and crashing into the side of your car. Just ask yourself how many times has it happened to you? You could say that when it did happen you were just unlucky. That could be true, because sometimes events happen around us that are out of our control. Then yes we can find ourselves in deep trouble without any warning. Just ask yourself how many times has something happened to you where you have been in great danger and where you had no warning at all? I'm forty years old and can only think of about 8 or 10 times and that's not counting my wedding day.

What this tells you is that you have a good insight into staying safe and are using good judgement and threat assessment. You are aware of your surroundings and have built up your own threat assessment warning system. I talked before about colour coding your level of awareness and that white is being switched off having no interest about what is going on around you. This is the prime time for something to happen. From you walking into a closed glass door, to someone seeing you are a target and an easy victim. Awareness of your personal safety is the single most important thing about staying safe anywhere. It is the quickest, easiest and most practical thing you can do to say safe. Too much time is spent on trying to teach people fighting skills, which are rendered useless in the heat of confrontation. Unless you are willing to train physically hard to make your self-more used to fighting, you will only be able to rely on your built in survival mechanism. So it makes sense to understand your awareness skills and how quickly you can feel when a situation is safe or a threat. Without it you are in the dark and a victim.

Remember:

1. If someone is in your personal space and is moving in closer and is not your lover THREAT.
2. If you see or feel that a situation is uncomfortable MOVE AWAY.
3. If someone asks you a question move back, if they come into your space THREAT.
4. If you feel unhappy about being in any situation or place LEAVE.
5. Always be switched on to your surroundings.

What would you do?

CHAPTER 3

FEAR

"Fear of confrontation can beat us, fear can make us believe that we are up against impossible odds, but it can give us strength and speed and its also our greatest ally. It is with us before, during and after a confrontation and ready to help us within a split second's notice."

Adrenaline is our body's natural defence mechanism it is our misinterpretation of the chemicals now following in our bloodstream that confuses adrenaline with fear. In fact, it can be argued that there is no such thing as fear. If we look at the dictionary definition of fear we find fear to be **'A feeling of distress, apprehension, or alarm caused by impending danger, pain, etc'.** We have been brought up to think of fear as something tangible, as something experienced only by weak people. When in fact, fear is only a description of the symptoms of adrenal release. Fear is such a negative concept because it promotes helplessness and helplessness is the last thing you want to be feeling when experiencing adrenaline because it will make you release even more.

Whenever we sense danger or confrontation be it real or imaginary our adrenal glands situated on the kidneys release a mixture of chemicals commonly know as adrenaline. Adrenaline is sometimes referred to, as the flight or fight drug, which can make you feel very uncomfortable indeed, but these feelings, cannot hurt you. Without over simplifying adrenaline can be experienced in two main forms, Anticipated and Unexpected. If we expect something unpleasant is going to happen our body will release adrenaline in order to prepare us for confrontation. The more unpleasant the experience the more adrenaline is released. Unfortunately our nervous system doesn't seem to differentiate between the anticipated physical confrontation and the non-physical event.

So we end up with the following:

Situation: Mad axe man running down the street towards you shouting, **"Kill! Kill!, Kill!"**
Your body's response is to release Adrenaline, your physical response is to run away, Marks out of 10 for you using up the adrenaline to run: 10 points
.

Situation: Get up to make a speech. Your body's response is to release Adrenaline. Your physical response is to hold a notebook and pen, Marks out of 10 to physically use up Adrenaline: Big Fat Zero.

I have listed just some of the effects you may experience when adrenaline is released. It is more than likely that you will have at some point in your life experienced several of the effects listed here. We are often told that if we have these feelings it is a sign that we are scared and weak. When in reality we are becoming faster, stronger, pain resistant and explosive.

Effects you may experience when adrenaline is released.

Short Term Effects

Butterflies in the stomach or Nausea
Increased heart rate
Sweating
Dry mouth
Shakes
Loss of colour in the skin
Tunnel vision
Gross motor skills become difficult to perform
Thinking becomes difficult as blood is drawn away from the brain
and directed to the major muscle groups
Your strength and speed increase
Your pain tolerance increases
Diarrhoea

Extreme (More likely with Adrenal Dump)

Paralysis - Being frozen to the spot
Possible loss of bowel and bladder control
Memory distortion
Auditory exclusion (Deafness)

Longer term

Loss of appetite
Insomnia
Fatigue
Depression
Loss of libido
Irritable Bowel Syndrome
General decline in health due to the above symptoms

Have you ever noticed that fear and excitement often display very similar symptoms, or even wondered why?

The answer is simple; they are one in the same! The only difference is our perception of the event. If we perceive a pleasant outcome we feel exited and if we perceive an unpleasant one we feel apprehension. This is why two people doing the same thing can have completely different reactions to the same situation. Imagine two people about to make a parachute jump for the first time. One may be exited by the prospect and the other scared shitless.

We need to remember two things: Firstly, our reaction to any situation depends not on the situation itself, but on our individual perception of it. Secondly, we can tolerate adrenal response and find our performance enhanced up to a certain point. After which we find our ability to function and perform in these conditions greatly reduced.

So ask yourself the following question: If I had the choice, would I prefer to feel scared or ready for action.

So why does it seem that some people cope with adrenaline and others do not?

"I'll be with you in one minute Mr.Jones, make yourself comfortable and help yourself to one of the magazines"

Everyone feels adrenaline, no exceptions. The only difference is the way we react to it, we control it or it controls us. In order to address this problem we need a way of lessening the negative impact of the adrenaline on our ability to handle high stress situations and the key word is DESENSITISATION.

Again this is something that we can all relate to, we have all been in a situation that at first has made us feel uncomfortable. If over time the situation is repeated each time we feel a little more at ease. I have found myself on this merry go-round many times. One particular situation has stayed with me for many years and just thinking about it can have me feeling the stress of the day still now. That was the first time I went to meet and train with Geoff Thompson and Peter Consterdine founders of the British Combat Association. I had read many of Geoff and Peter's articles in the martial arts press and their books and seen their videos on training and self-defence. I contacted them and they invited me to come and train with them on their next course, which was in about 4 weeks time.

For the next month I was a nervous wreck, I had every feeling positive and negative you could imagine. I had the excitement of wanting to meet them and the fear of what if I am not good enough to handle the training. Before I go on with this story take a look at the list of the effects of adrenaline release again and let me tell you I felt every bloody one.

I must have read the letter Peter had sent me about the course and the directions of how to find them 20 times. When the day arrived I woke up in plenty of time; my training bag packed from the night before was being checked again for the fifth time that morning. I remember putting my coffee cup down and looking at the palms of my hands sweating, then having to visit the toilet again.

Fear can have you feeling out of control

I thought to myself that I'm not ready. May be it would be better if I went to the next training session, give myself a bit more time to get used to the idea. Crap, if I was in this state after 4 weeks what would I be like if I left it any longer? In the car for the off I checked my bag, letter and directions one more time. The journey took forever, and with every mile nearer the desire to turn off at the next junction and turn around and go back home got stronger. By the time I pulled into the car park of the leisure centre where the course was to be held I was a nervous wreck. I went into the reception area and asked where the BCA course was being held. They told me to go through to the gymnasium at the end of the corridor and go through to the canteen area. I felt like the condemned man going to the gallows. Looking into the canteen I could see about 25 to 30 guys every one of which looked to me as if they were all hardened street fighters. That was it, my bottle had hit the limit, I turned and walked back to the car park. Fear had griped me by the neck and was taking me back to the car. Remember this was something that I had wanted to do, train with the two people I had admired for a long time. I felt sick with myself for feeling so scared, that I was about to drive all the way back to London. What about all the people I had told about this weekend how would I face them? *"How was the course Alan"? "Well sorry guys I could not do it in the end".* Why? Could I tell them the truth? *"Well lads, its because I shit myself in the car park in Coventry".* I don't know how much adrenaline was running though my body in that car park, but if you could turn it into electricity you could have powered the Christmas lights in Oxford Street for a week.

I slammed the car door and went in to meet the enemy head on. I felt like I was walking with the speed and power of a freight train. Sure in the fact that if I stopped moving forward for one second I would be on my way back to London. Within a short time I was talking to people and introduced myself to Peter and Geoff who made me feel so welcome. I think they could see how scared I looked and took pity on the fat Londoner.

And one of the hard face street fighters turned out to be a soft hearted puppy by the name of Darrin Richardson and our friendship has grown stronger from that first day. So if I had given into the feeling to turn around and go back home on that day. I would never have met some of the people who have done and given me so much over the last eight years. As for the idea of meeting up with the guys now, I still get the adrenaline but it's excitement not fear or weakness.

Everyone can relate to the story of being anxious about going to or meeting someone for the first time. From a new job to taking a driving test. All of us feel easier after the event and as time passes it fades more and more. We have all felt adrenalin so start working on the idea that you cannot stop the body giving you this rush. And look at it as something that will get you through whatever has turned your body's adrenal switch on. It may be hard to understand the sudden rush that can hit us when we are confronted by someone's aggression. Fear of what is about to happen or what could happen will stop most people from doing anything about the situation at the time. Like most things we need to practise and understand the feeling and that sometimes things can and do go wrong.

A game plan and an understanding of what we are likely to feel and believe to be happening to us at the time is needed. Our fear of a situation is a danger only if we do not understand the feeling.

So what is going on?

Why do we get this overwhelming urge to run or shake all over? Why do we feel so weak with just the thought of confrontation, or a physical challenge?

If I put you into a room with a rabid dog your overriding urge would be to run, and get out of the room as fast as possible. If I stood you outside that room, and told you that in one minute you would have to go in and confront the dog, for the next 60 seconds you would be thinking of all the places that dog is going to bite you. The feeling to run would get stronger with every tick of the clock; the urge to run is basic survival. To go into a room and to let a dangerous animal confront you, and to stay there because some one told you to is ridiculous. The point is, being confronted or the thought of confrontation brings on the same feelings inside. You feel uncomfortable and you want to get out or not to go in. If you were unaware of the danger, and the dog suddenly confronts you, the shock you feel is intense for a few seconds you are frozen to the spot and vulnerable.

So what is going on? What are we feeling and why do we want to run?

We want to run, because the instinct to run kept our ancestors alive for thousands of years. So take yourself back a few hundred thousand years, imagine yourself as a caveman: great fun no tax to pay, living off the land, no boss, the fear of marriage is something that's not going to be invented for a long time yet. Just eating and sleeping and no one telling you how or what to feel, if you find yourself in danger you can just run away. Later you meet up with your fellow cavemen and tell them how an angry bear confronted you and you ran away from danger as quickly as you could. They pat you on the back and say *"ug, gooler ug fug ballor ug"!* Or *"Well done mate you don't want to fuck around with a big angry bear".*

To run is our strongest instinct to get away from danger and the one natural instinct modern man tries so hard to cover up. When we get the feeling today because of our social conditioning we hold it back. We will not go with this natural response because we have been told it's a weakness. Because we misinterpret this natural feeling we only add to the problem. We do not like it, we feel we are weak because of the feeling to run. We feel out of control of ourselves. Because we do not fully understand what is going on inside us this only adds to our misinterpretation and the feeling gets worse.

The caveman did not give a monkey's about what people thought about him because the feeling of fear was in the open. If something attacked you, you killed it and ate it, if something scared you, you ran. Ok we can't run from our boss when he gives us a job we don't like or kill the person who talks behind us in the cinema. This is the modern world with its entire array of dos and don'ts but the caveman's instinct is still inside us. We have to take steps to understand, control and use this powerful and natural resource.

Why do we get such a strong physical reaction to something that we cannot touch or see?

It may be difficult to see how something can so strongly override our feelings. Something we cannot see yet can have us shaking in the corner or running faster than we thought possible. Things happen in the body all the time without us having conscious thoughts about them. From our heartbeat to breathing when we sleep. It may help to look at the effect as a more common drug. Look at it this way, if you went out to a bar and ordered a beer as you drink your first pint you know the alcohol in the beer is going to enter your bloodstream. Over time, the more you drink the more alcohol will get into your body. You know that at this rate by the end of the night you are going to be feeling all the mental and physical effect of the alcohol. Poor vision, your feeling of being more attractive to the opposite sex and your legs unable to understand the basic principles of walking. Your thought processes go on a roller-coaster ride as you struggle to understand why the tall good looking plant at the end of the bar doesn't want to dance with you.

Before you started to drink you know that the chemicals are in the beer, you do not have to understand the molecular structure of the alcohol. Just that it's in the beer. As the chemicals build up they will affect the way your brain operates. So you know that what is going on inside your mind is a chemical exchange, and will affect your physical movement and your mental judgement. Because we understand and are familiar with the effects of alcohol, we are happy to deal with the good and bad side of the chemicals running through our body.

Pre-fight fear can make us feel weak and unable to fight before anything physical has started. But how many of us work to understand why we feel pre-fight fear and how we can use it and not look upon it as a weakness? Like alcohol the larger the amount the greater the effect. Now I know for most of us just holding a pint of beer will not bring us out in a cold sweat, for most of us it's part of a enjoyable night out. Because we understand the way the drink will affect us, we are happy to enjoy it and for most of us we can control the intake. Because we recognise the effects we feel comfortable and happy to enjoy the affects of the alcohol.

The key to coping with adrenaline is keeping it within manageable levels.

If we experience adrenal release over our limit, we cannot cope and cease to function properly. We experience symptoms such as being frozen to the spot or talking rapidly and incoherently. In this state we cannot deal with any situation we may find ourselves in. Just walking down a dark street or someone just looking at you the wrong way can automatically bring on an involuntary rush of adrenalin. Most people when confronted with an aggressive attacker will back down with the shock of being verbally attacked. Your heart races, your limbs shake and you feel an uncontrollable urge to find a toilet. All this and you still haven't decided what technique you're going to use to get away from this guy.

I have trained with and seen some fantastic martial artists. And I have also worked with people on the doors of night-clubs who have never trained in the martial arts, yet are more prepared for the reality of a street fight. Not because they know more fighting techniques, it's because night after night they are feeling and controlling the affects of their adrenaline.

Like I said about being aware of your situation and going with the feeling, if you feel uncomfortable, get away. Adrenalin will make you feel uncomfortable and in most situations will have you feeling that it's time to go before you can understand why. Keeping the feeling within manageable levels like the doorman of a club controls the feeling by facing it night after night. You can do the same.

NO DON'T STOP READING, COME BACK. I'm not saying you have to go up to the Gorilla standing on the door of a night club and ask if you can have his job. We just have to get you to try out something that brings on a rush of adrenalin so you can recognise how your body reacts. If you find out the hairs on your neck stand on end or your mouth is as dry as the desert, you can recognise and learn to control the feeling. For me confrontation hits me in the left leg and the hairs on the back of my neck stand on end. It's so bad if I had long hair I would look like Don King. If the situation has developed into a dangerous situation my left leg shakes so bad that I have to make the conscious effort to lock it out and force my heel into the ground. Someone seeing me rubbing the back of my neck or controlling the movements of my leg could see me as someone who is scared, or as someone in need of a hospital. I have sometimes thought to myself what if I let my left leg do what it wanted to do and let it run off. Would my right leg follow? Or would it stay which would result in me being ripped in two by an inpatient left leg, and leaving me lying on the pavement looking like a 20stone hamburger?

Remember the same feeling of adrenal release would be felt on a roller coaster ride with the anticipation of what's going to happen. As you feel the click, click, click of the car being pulled up the start ramp of the ride, your heart pounding, your hands are sweating and the hairs on your neck are standing up. Fear, fun or excitement; which would you be feeling at this point?

It's the way we interpret the feeling about a situation that will give us the answer. If these reactions are mistaken for fear, the cycle of self-doubt has started. But if you get used to feeling and reacting to them you can take control and accept that these feelings are natural. Don't jump in with both feet, take it one step at a time, start small and build up. Each success brings greater control. For years you may have wanted to do something like join a dance or theatre class at your local collage but you have felt uneasy about going. What will people say, what if the people there are better than you are. So what? Be a caveman who cares what they think. Its more than likely the people who have been doing the classes for sometime will be better than you. But they all started with that first step of walking through the door. You know this is right. You have been in situations where you have had to welcome people into situations that they are new to. From the work place in helping someone to find their way around and telling them who does what.

Adrenalin will give you doubt free of charge, but you pay for it by staying in the same place doing nothing and feeling a victim.

This is not a book about understanding all the stresses adrenalin can bring into our lives it's about staying safe on the street. There are some great books out there that deal with the subject in better and greater detail than I can in one book about self protection. I have recommended some in the back of this book, so if this chapter has left you wanting to know more get them and read more. I'm sure they will help you as much as they helped me.

Coping with the physical effects.

Apart from the freeze factor when confrontation comes knocking at your door, the physical effects of tunnel vision and loss of gross motor skills are the ones that stand out when having to do something physical to protect yourself. I will talk about this in greater detail in later chapters but as these effects are coursed by adrenalin let's take a quick look at them now.

Tunnel Vision

When someone is attacked they may say they did not see their attacker before the person attacked them. In most situation's it's because the person was not aware of their surroundings. This is not tunnel vision; only being able to focus on one thing and being blind to anything outside that range is tunnel vision. With the danger in front of you your brain will have you focus on that because it sees that as the danger. The stronger the confrontation the stronger you will be locked in.

Try this little test, look straight ahead and bring your arm out in front of you. If you are reading this on a train you may like to wait until you get home or see if the other passengers would like to try it out with you. Now keeping your arms at chest height bring both arms behind your back, keep looking forward and stop when you can no longer see your hands. Now keep looking forward slowly bring your hands forward and wiggle your fingers. As soon as you see the fingers wiggling in the corner of your eye stop. This is your field of vision. Your moving fingers are picked up by your peripheral vision so you can take in a lot of visual information. Now bring your hands back in front of you until your thumbs touch, now look at the distance between your two little fingers and that's all you would have to work with if you had tunnel vision.

So if the person in front of you decided to attack you by stabbing you in the belly you would not see it. Nor would you see his mate who was coming in on your blind side to attack you. Tunnel vision is something that you have to learn to deal with when confronted and we will look at it in greater detail later.

Gross Motor Skills

Loss of gross motor skills or losing the ability to do anything physically complicated when you are under the effects of adrenalin. Again we are back to basic levels here if you like back to the caveman. Because I'm sorry to say it my friends that when life threatening danger is knocking at your door, you're going to be fighting with the side of your brain that is still rooted in prehistoric times. So the muscles that you can use to defend yourself with are for running away or clubbing your attacker to bits. Something as stressful as the fear, of an attack will make your hands, legs and feet work on a basic level. If you like stress makes you more clumsy than the proverbial bull in a china shop. Or if you have ever been in a rush to open your front door because you can hear the telephone ringing and found yourself fumbling with the keys you will know what I mean, stress makes us clumsy.

So if you have been on a self-defence course that had you breaking free of a hold and sending your attacker flying in the air, in a real situation with the pressure greater than you trying to get indoors to answer a phone call, it won't work. We will look at the idea of what you can do to fight back later and what you should be practising to make your attack workable. But there is a big difference between workable and what people think they could do to fight back, you could look at it like this.

Imagine someone training in the fighting arts with kicks and punches that take great skill and many years of practise to perfect. With all these years of training this person has more defence and attack combinations you could fit in a shelf full of books. But put him outside on a warm summer's day eating a plate of Jam sandwiches and a wasp decides he likes the look of the Jam. The highly trained fighter will go back to the basics and automatically wave his hands and arms from side to side and jog up and down on the spot. In a stressful situation only basic movements work, your ingrained gross motor skills kick in and any thing complicated will be taken away by the rush of adrenaline.

Like I said in the opening to this chapter "Fear of confrontation can beat us, fear can make us believe that we are up against impossible odds". Someone with the greatest fighting skills possible without understanding how they are going to feel and train to understand and recognise the problem. They will not be able to take advantage of the rest of this quote.

"But it can give us strength and speed and it's also our greatest ally". It is with us before, during and after a confrontation and ready to help us within a split second's notice."

CHAPTER 4

Consequence

We have all been faced with the problem of having to deal with the consequences of our actions. From a violent situation to may be saying the wrong thing at the wrong time to a loved one. It is something that comes up more than once or twice in just a 24 hour day; we make thousands of judgements a day. Many of which have good or bad consequences, it's just part of our day to day lives. If you are late for work, do you run for the train and put yourself in danger of all the possible consequences? From falling down the steps to the platform, or doing your best 100 metres dash only to have the train doors close in your face. Filled with frustration you kick the departing train only to end up with the pain of a badly broken toe, now you are late for work and in pain.

This may read like something from a Fawlty Tower's script. But I'm sure every one of you can think of a situation you have been in where you wish you could have had a second chance or a free replay of a situation. We cannot change the past or a situation that turned out bad for us, but we can learn a great deal from it. Most of us will be faced with the fear of confrontation and the biggest thing that stops us from doing something positive or physical about it is the fear of consequence. "If I punch this guy what if he doesn't fall down?" "Look at the size of him, if I hit him with my best punch it's just going to bounce off and he will kill me". "If I hit him first, the police will be knocking on my door. And in the morning they will take me down the cells for a friendly chat about why I attacked the said gentleman, who is also pressing charges against me. He picked the fight with me! He was the one threatening to give me a new face, now he's taking me to court. What a joke, should I have let him kick the hell out of me?"
Some of this may have a familiar ring. The amazing thing is that all this is going though your head, and before any punch has landed on anyone's jaw or a kick has made it's home into someone else's groin.

Your fear of the possible outcome to a situation can delay your reactions. You could be in line for the beating of your life as all the consequences of the situation flash though your head like an express train. The point must be made that in no way do you have to get physical to win a potentially dangerous situation. It is stronger to walk away and let the other person off and to ignore all of the verbal attacks. If you wake up the next morning with the same good looking face you had when you went to bed you won. It is a hard pill to swallow, but do you really need all the possible comebacks. More to the point, could you handle them if they did? For me I have found over the years, it's the fear of consequence that has always been the hardest part for me to handle within street confrontation. I may have my own way of dealing with it now. But it's taken a long time and many sleepless nights, to get to grips with my feelings, and accepting the fact that my personal fears will raise their ugly head with every confrontation I may be faced with. Only now can I accept them and handle the consequences, but it's still there every time. What is important to understand is that we all feel the feeling and it's normal.

We can all fantasize about what we would do in a real confrontation. But when the fear of a real situation hits you, you will be amazed at the mental and physical logjam you will find yourself trapped in, with any logical breakdown of the situation going out the window. To give you some idea, what do you make of this situation: Having to get out of my car to confront (sorry talk to) a fellow motorist who had been driving like a twat and after eye contact though the windscreen was no longer content to stay in his car. Within seconds I was face to face with this guy who was now screaming in my face and using words with one syllable like they were going out of fashion. After the usual come on let's go, and think your hard comments, we came to the stand off.

As I lined him up with a punch that would have had him eating though a straw for a good six weeks, I was hit by consequence. We were both now standing on the pavement. What follows is just a part of my normal thought process going into overdrive. Mental logjam, losing your bottle, fear of getting hurt, not confident that what you know will work or fear of consequence, call it what you like.

Like I said before, consequence has been my biggest battle to get to grips with. Ok back to the fistfight at the north London corral. I had him lined up, confidant that my punch would send him to sleep, when BANG! What could be the consequences of me hitting him? As always, it hit me harder than a punch in the guts. What if I do hit him, it could be so hard that he may fall back into traffic. Say one of the oncoming cars had to crossover the road and drive into the oncoming traffic to miss the now unconscious body lying in the road. Say one of the unsuspecting drivers was driving a school bus full of children returning from a swimming lesson. Now the school bus driver loses control and ends up driving off the road and over a bridge and crashes onto the railway tracks below. Not all the children are killed, thank God. But wait; now I can imagine the oncoming train and no way will it have time to stop. As the train hits the school bus the train driver and the remaining children are killed. As the fireball engulfs the bridge I can see the last car of the train is carrying nuclear waste. With the force of the crash the train explodes, atoms are split and 20 miles of London is laid to waste. The governments of the world pick up the explosion on their satellites and believing it to be an attack push the button. *"Oh my God!"*
So World War 3 starts because I have to hit this guy because he drives like a twat and now feels he has to get physical.

Now you may be thinking the guy writing this must be on some type of mind-expanding drug. No. This is the type of thing that can go though your mind when confronted with a potentially dangerous situation. I may have been a bit colourful in my example, but your fears will make you think and make you believe that you are in a no win situation. The physical part is easy; the hard part is training yourself to commit the punch, and to do it before the feeling of consequence takes hold. It may not be events at the time; you could have the feeling for a long time afterwards. As time goes on you feel the greater the comeback, *"ok if I do knock this guy out what if he comes back later and throws a petrol bomb though my kitchen window when I'm having breakfast?"*

Like many people, for me the "what if"? question was the one that went around in my head for days after any confrontation. If you have been in any type of street or club confrontation I'm sure you can understand the point I am trying to make. That the main battle is with yourself, not just the guy in front of you. To you he may also look like he is built out of the hardest substance known to man. But that again is something you are putting together in your own head. Before he takes it any further you are the one who has convinced yourself that you are in a no win situation, you've lost the fight before the fight has begun. Again you may think that the story about World War 3 starting because of one punch is pushing the boat out just a little bit too far. But if you have ever been face to face with violence I'm sure you can relate to the way your mind can and does play amazing tricks on you. Remember I'm not talking about all the effects of adrenaline here, you have to add this to the picture as well. No wonder people can fall apart. Not only do you have the thug in front of you, but also you are attacking yourself with weapons more powerful than any punch or kick the thug may have.

How can we work out our fears and start to deal with the fact that we all have them. There are no exceptions. We all feel it from a Librarian to a seasoned street fighter, because one of them deals with the feelings on a regular basis they begin to control it. So it's exposure that makes one handle it better than the other one does. The reality of it is that without understanding and accepting the fact that you have to strengthen your mental physique as well as any physical techniques to deal with a confrontation, you are training for only part of the story. It maybe harder than all the hard physical training you may put yourself through to win a kick-boxing contest or a judo black belt grading. But without putting yourself though your personal fears and getting to grips with them you are working from a weak base line.

Most people believe you have to conquer fear. Wrong, you feel it, control it and use it. Training to understand your fear is like any other, if you do not practise feeling it, how do you expect to control it? All of us will have this battle every time we are confronted with a situation. To deal with it we have to accept that it happens and we have to expose ourselves to the feeling as much as we can to get used to it.

If you are confronted out of the blue, you will be engaged in a mental battle straight away and the longer it goes on the worse it will get, from knocking him unconscious to dreaming up World War 3 only takes a second. Within just a few seconds you can fall apart. You cannot look at situations as a set piece: if he grabs me I will do this, if he throws a punch I will hit him, wrong! You will be too late. If you cannot control the feeling that is now running though your body quicker than last night's curry and lager, you will run out of time.

So how can we train and prepare ourselves to handle consequence? Make part of your training reflect the reality of a street fight. Getting your training partner to add verbal attacks as well as punches and kicks to your fighting drills can help. The adrenal reaction you get from such training will give you a good insight into how your body will react to adrenaline. But consequence is something that only you can interpret. I mean your worst idea of an outcome will be different to my own. But if you take the worst case scenario you can work back to find the point at which you personally are happy to deal with a situation.

If you are not confident with your physical ability you can work out a good part of this doubt with training. Just feeling how hard you can hit a pad can give you a great boost. If you find yourself saying, "Oh No, not this drill I hate it, I can't do it" then that's the drill that will help you to build your mental physique. It doesn't matter if you are crap at a particular training drill; the fact that you push yourself to get on the mat builds your ability to control your fears and handle the consequences of looking bad in front of other people.

If you know you hit hard you will have the confidence to use it

One question I get asked a lot at seminars is: *"What about the law if you use a pre-emptive attack?"* This is consequences at it's best and my normal answer would be *"Who cares? Yes, you should know your rights. But the person in front of you could stab you in the neck as you are thinking over the legal consequences".* Again you are loading yourself down, putting more weight on your shoulders. Your fear of consequence is the same as you carrying heavy suitcases. People keep adding to the weight but only you can carry them. And only you can drop them.

With more and more baggage you will be less and less able to handle what is going on around you. The Police and Courts lay down the law and they do have a difficult job to do. And if you are wronged in some way they have the power to help get you justice. And Yes, I know many people who have dealt with a situation and ended up having to give an account of themselves in court. But they are alive and able to plead their case. Maybe if they had held onto the legal baggage longer, they would not be standing in a courtroom, but laying six feet under. How's that for a worst case scenario? When face to face with danger in the street you are the one who has to deal with it. Your attacker could not give a monkey's about any legal consequences; just if he beats the crap out of you will he have time to get back to the pub for last orders. Anyway consequences has 4 syllables.

It's up to you to set the level at which you would use force. For me, I look at it like this: there is no grey area, I am fighting or I'm not fighting. I have found that giving myself a personal set of levels at which to gauge when I will get physical has helped me handle my fears of consequence. Most of the levels deal with the situation before it gets to a stand off. Basic awareness and threat assessment techniques play a large part. As this is all going on, I am dealing with the feelings and bad images that are going though my mind. I know my fears. I have had them attack me many times, so if I'm willing to deal with my worst-case scenario the possible fight in front of me becomes less of a problem. Adding to the positive, I tell myself *"Whatever the outcome of this situation, it is NOT possible for my worst case scenario to come true here today"*,

With all this going on to throw a punch is hard when you are thinking of everything that could happen. Your arms and legs feel they are full of lead shot. I found that for years my training was not helping me with the hard facts of what happens in the 10 seconds before a fight kicks off. Having the skills was ok in the club when I was training. But it never happens like that in the street. I was waiting for it to happen before I pulled out the gun so to speak, which left me no time to get my finger on the trigger. The key was to set myself a level at which I could throw a punch and would not be affected by the mental logjam, finding an automatic trigger to override the logjam and fire.

Thinking more about the possible outcome and trying to understand it was doing me no good. I mean if someone is going to attack you, and you have done everything possible to get away from the situation, if you then go back and try and renegotiate and try to think about the logic of the situation, you mentally hit a brick wall. Don't look for logic, I mean where's the logic in someone stabbing someone over a spilt pint of beer.

When someone is threatening you and you can smell his breath in your face, the more you look for logic you just end up giving yourself a mental beating. To override this when a situation gets to your fight level you attack. This should be the same feeling as someone sticking you with a pin. Your muscles work on reflex. No thinking, just action. The good thing about setting levels and working from the idea that your attack is triggered from a level you set beforehand, helps you take the lead. But you have to train the trigger with the strike. We will look in detail in a later chapter on how to train and work striking with triggers. So let's look a bit more at consequences.

The monster at the door

We all feel the consequence monster banging on the door and the more we fear the outcome the more the monster hits the door. We can find ourselves unable to move for fear of making the situation worse.

Holding back the fear of consequences

We can experience so much in such a short space of time that the mind boggles with just how far we can go within our own heads. The fear we have about the outcome to a situation is strong, not just for you but for your loved ones. We send ourselves spinning along a mental motorway journey with thousands of dangers and possible outcomes. I have been on this journey many times myself and not all of them have been to do with the threat of violence. Like I said before consequence has been my baggage for a long time.

As I mentioned before I was a bouncer back in the 80's. And as any doorman will tell you the threat of comebacks is a regular occurrence. One club I worked in was a small nightclub with good regular customers and a good atmosphere and you could not call it a hard club to work. You got the run of the mill problems with small groups, but on the whole if there ever was a nice place to work as a doorman this was it. But for me it turned out to have one night handmade for me. The four guys that came in together that night seemed fine. Normally four guys together would have the doorman take an extra look, and we did but all looked fine.

Who, why and how it kicked off no one was sure, but it did. How we got the four guys (who had looked ok at the start of the evening) back to the main door is hard to remember. When you hear there's a problem you just go in. One of the victims of the trouble was on the floor with his back against the bar, his hands covering his face with his blood coming through the gaps in his fingers. That's about all I can remember about the fight that broke out until we ended up at the main door. The main door to the club was a solid wooden door with two toughened glass windows, both about the size of a piece of A5 paper. The door opened outwards on to the street. The reception area was closed off from the rest of the club by two double doors. The area between the doors was about the size of a large family bathroom. Me, another doorman, the club manager and the four now very aggressive guys were packed into the reception area tighter than sardines in a tin. I don't think a punch was thrown because no one had room to do a thing. The guy I had hold of was right in front of me. We were face-to-face and so close you could not have passed a fag paper between us. He was older than the normal visitors to the club say late 30's early 40's. The shouting and abuse coming from his mates was deafening and I remember thinking what's taking so long, why hasn't someone got the outer door open.

The guy in front of me said nothing. He just looked at me and in a way that would freeze water. And out of the blue just his look had me thinking about my bowel movements. He did not shout, he just said quietly that when he got out of here he would come back and blow my knees off. With that the latch-bar on the outer door was lifted and the pressure we had built up inside forced very one out on to the street. With some pushing and some goodbye swearing we got back into the club and once the door was closed we could breath again. A bang on the door had me look through the glass. There was my friend who could freeze water, he was holding an imaginary shotgun. Pointing it at me through the glass in the door, lowering the gun to about knee height he pulled the imaginary trigger. Then pointing his finger at me he mouthed the words, *"I will see you later"*.

Like I said before you get people telling you what they are going to do when you are on your way home or they will comeback next week with a load of mates. Drink and bullshit talking normally, but this guy had got to me. On my way home that night I was like a frightened rabbit. When I got home and to the safety of my bed the fear was still with me, what if he's followed me home? It was a week before I was going to work back at that club. I found out that a week has 14 days, and the days last 48 hours, this guy had switched on my fear of consequence and I was a mess.

I suppose the old saying of sticks and stones may break my bones but names will never hurt me, to some point is true. If you only look at it as a physical beating, but names and threats are what most of us find hard to deal with. We beat ourselves with the fear of consequence.

Seeing it happen before it does

Not all my problems with consequence are to do with violence. Like many parents out there dealing with just making sure the kids stay safe is a big one. The same as paying the bills and the rent or mortgage, if I don't get the money for this then that may happen. Depending on what you fear and what you perceive the outcome to be that keeps you adding more and more problems. You are the one feeding the monster and the

If you don't control the monster it just gets bigger

monster makes you unable to do something or unwilling to try. Just how quickly you can see a problem or danger of the possible outcome of a situation is also dealing with and fearing consequence.

Children can put you though this easily and the number of times my children have had me running to catch them. Or had me moving things out of their way so as not to have them fall over, fall on, fall flat, trip, smash or kill themselves with an electrical appliance, must run into the thousands. I can see the whole thing in a flash. From my son playing in the back garden, happily playing out a scene from Star Wars and giving Darth Vader a good kicking with his light-sabre. He runs back into the house to get some more weapons to help him with the battle to save the universe. He trips on one of his toys sending him out of control toward the glass panelled back door. By the time he has got back his footing I have seen the consequences. The glass breaking his face and body cut to pieces and rushing to the hospital, all the phone calls I would have to make telling the grandparents what happened. Should I call an ambulance or would I be better of fighting my way through London traffic? Have I got petrol, will the car start, should I lock up the house or just go? TEA! I've left the BLOODY KETTLE ON I better turn that off or the house could burn down when we're at the hospital.

As I fall to the floor with my third imaginary heart attack that day, my son opens the kitchen door and turns to me and asks are you all right Dad? My son did not crash through the glass door, just like the man who could freeze water never came back to the club.

I have come to the point that I can deal with the consequence of violence because I will not let the feeling come into the picture. I will do anything not to be drawn into a fight. I will only kick off with someone if I really have to. If I have no choice I will do anything to win, because my reasons when to fight are greater than the consequences not to.

I know how long and hard I struggled with my fears of consequence. The first step is to understand that we all have them and it is not because you are weak. It is normal to have these feelings. All my training now pushes me to my limits and I test myself every time I train. I make it feel as real as I can and this gives me the confidence that I can deal with a real confrontation. Every effort should always be made to get away from confrontation, but if you can't your training should reflect what really can happen. Some of my comments about how I deal with confrontation now, you may have found a bit over the top but for me it works. A good friend of mine once said to me about the fear of a possible outcome to a situation *"Alan, you have got to be alive to go to prison"*.

Every one of us has a consequence monster and every day it knocks on the door. Our judgements about the situation can keep control over how hard it knocks. But if your life is threatened bolt the bloody door and survive.

Chapter 5

Fighting Back Who For?

We can all relate to how someone or something has had us feeling powerless, or unable to do anything about a situation. It must come from our overwhelming urge to move away from conflict, but everyday we are faced with something. Who's going to make the dinner, or who told the boss that you took an extra half an hour for lunch? All switch on our fight or flight response and have us feeling the internal conflict. Of maybe throwing the dinner at the wall, giving the boss' informer chocolate cake filled with laxative.

As individuals we all have our own start button when it comes to reacting to situations. You may feel life is too short to think and worry about how you are going to look after yourself in a street fight. So much more is going on in your life, that to keep adding more and more levels of complexity to your ever-decreasing life span may seem a waste of time. I mean you may never have the chance to use the information. You may never be attacked in your whole life so why bother? In fact the Sun will burn out in a few million years so why bother about anything?

As with most things in life it's our choice as to what we see as a priority. But, like being a passenger in a car crash or finding your holiday flight to the sun is about to make a crash landing into the sea, situations can change around us that are out of your control and so do your priorities. From earthquakes, floods, tornadoes and volcanoes erupting to murders, rapes, muggings and brutal knife attacks. They all carry a degree of probability; they have all happen, but not to everyone. But we all come into contact with situations that can develop into a very dangerous problem and without us understanding the build up. It can explode in your face larger and quicker than you ever felt possible. So the answer to who for? Is for yourself. It's your choice. No one is going to force you to do anything.

But because you are reading this book you have an interest and with that interest comes a spark of knowledge that can help you stay safer on the streets.

All Alone

Most of us do a good job of staying out of trouble. Just think about the millions of people who go through their daily routine and find they are dealing with situations every day. Most of us understand the feeling of a particular situation maybe getting out of control and dealing with it by saying. "Sorry, it was my fault let me buy you another drink" or "Excuse me I'm sorry about that, can I help?" We have all made excuses for someone else or apologised when something was not our fault, but it kept us in control of a situation.
It is when outside influences, drink, drugs or the type of day that the person had can change the situation. Understanding that someone can change out of their normal character and become an uncontrollable monster with just a bit of drink and a bad day at work. By the time they meet you in the pub or walk past you in the street just the smallest thing is going to set them off. One thing is for sure, you're on your own, you could be in a pub full of people or a shopping centre that's as busy as the pre Christmas rush, But a violent situation directed at you would be privately yours; no one will come forward to help you. With a sea of people around you, you will have to deal with the situation on your own.

Most people do not want to get involved with a situation that could turn on them and many will feel glad that the person has picked on someone else. If the place is full of people this makes it easier for others to walk away because they pass on the idea of helping the victim out to all the other people around them. "Someone else will help" "They must know each other" "If I step in he could attack me, anyway the police will be here in a minute."

I have found this out so many times. People will hand over any responsibility within a crowd. Some friends and I were having a day at the coast and being a bank holiday thousands of others had the same idea. We visited the local amusement park and apart from the queuing we were having a great time. Someone in the queue noticed smoke coming from a part of the park. Within no time people were running and from that end of the park, one of my friends said we should call 999.

The rest of us turned and said they will be on their way, someone would have called the fire brigade. My friend still went off to find a phone box. He called the emergency services and to his amazement no call had been made about a fire at the park. By the time the services got to the park the ride was burning like crazy, no one was killed or hurt in the fire. But if someone had been trapped in the fire they could have died because of the crowd believing someone else would help or phone for help.

Some years ago I was out for a meal with a friend. The restaurant was packed and why not, it was Saturday night and a good restaurant. We were sitting enjoying a drink and coffee after a great meal when there was a problem at the entrance. Having glass doors that looked right into the restaurant I could see the receptionist was having trouble with 3 guys. Within a few seconds the manager and one of the kitchen staff had come to see what was going on, and help the girl on reception. Tempers were getting shorter and the volume was getting louder. The guys must have just left the pub and seeing a light on must have thought that they could pack some more beer into their already swollen bladders. The shouting turned to pushing and the conversation the guys were having was on a level you would think came from 3 walking cans of beer. *"Sod this, what a way to end an evening"* I said to my friend. Remember the restaurant was full of people, all could see and hear the problem. Most moaned about it, many looked away, but no one did anything to help.

No I do not see myself as John Wayne, walking into a western town to save the townspeople from the bad guys. You can look at it in two ways, one these guys were ruining a great evening for me and I was just pissed off, or two it was getting out of hand and the danger of them about to start throwing things (apart from punches)

I felt was real. The guys wanted a drink and were taking it out on the staff.

They were not attacking me, just spoiling part of my evening. I walked up and opened the doors into the reception area; my plan was to put forward my case of feeling that they were ruining my evening. I hoped they would see me as some member of the public who was out with his girlfriend. And no matter how much they shouted at me, they would see that I was not responsible for refusing to serve them a drink. This was my plan and that's what I told them, the matter was over and less of a problem I thought it would be.

The guys could see my side, in fact only 1 out of the 3 wanted more beer and soon his mates had convinced him to take part in another Saturday night favourite, finding a kebab shop.

Ok you can say that I put myself in danger and you're right. But the point of this example is to see that most people do not help out. The restaurant was full and when the problem started the girl on the reception was on her own. If it had kicked off then I would have been in the deep end, but I accepted that when I opened the door to help. If I had sat there it still could have kicked off. But also I felt that someone other than a member of the restaurant staff could have a more calming influence. I was taking a risk, I was helping out, and I was showing off to the girlfriend, I was stupid, but the free coffee and Brandy from the management showed they were pleased with my choice.

Someone once told me how they came to the aid of a woman who was being hit by what turned out to be her boyfriend. When he said to the guy, *"Look mate stop hurting the lady"* the guy turned on him and punched him to the floor and started to kick him. The woman, who had been the person the guy had wanted to help, now also turned on him and joined in with the kicking. The pub was full but the guy on the floor was alone. Again this story and many others like it you could fill a library with and people will switch off to it after a time. I mean how shocking can stories be, when you hear it over and over or refuse to listen.

Having looked after my children for the last 9 years this has put me in a high state of awareness (AND STRESS) as to their safety. Forever looking out for them, I may have pissed a few family members off with my worries about their and my children's safety. But I can't turn that side of me off. As my children get older they will find themselves dealing with the problems that confront us all. But with the sick-minded people that are out there that will pick on children, I have to do all I can to look out for them. You could say that this would be the worse thing that could happen to them: being taken by someone. Add all the other things like crossing the road to safety in the home, as the parents we should look out for danger all the time. Ok we may not be fighting off an attacker every day, but we are on the look out for problems and keeping our loved ones safe. I am forty years old and my Mum still sees me as her little boy, some things you never stop doing.

Who For?

I have had hundreds of people come and train with me over the years and from different backgrounds and with different fighting skills. But most find it hard to understand the hard and brutal face of violence, and that some people find pleasure from inflicting pain on others. Most people look for striking skills, from punches to kicks, grappling skills from standing to floor to protect them against an attacker. But only a handful would understand if I just ran at them shouting, *"Who are you looking at? What the fuck are you going to do?"* As I simulate pushing a screwdriver into their chest.

Because you are reading this then the, "who" is you (try saying that 10 times after a couple of drinks) and only you can make the choice. Again what I have been saying so far is that most situations can be avoided with awareness and threat assessment.

The fighting part is a small part of the picture. But hard to deal with if you are not prepared to see the reality of just how brutal it can be. You can fight for yourself, a loved one or the unknown victim it's your choice. But with the physical part of fighting back only being when you have no choice.

With nowhere to go

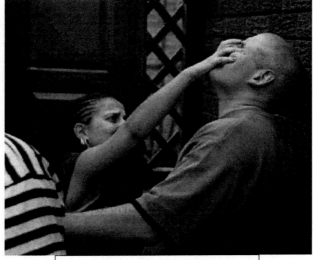

Flight is no longer an option

Chapter 6

IT WON'T WORK WITHOUT A TRIGGER

No, you are not going to read something about how to make your own gun with a toilet roll and some sticky back plastic. More to the point if you did have a gun on your person and were being attacked at what point would you use it? Many people have found themselves victims not because they were weaker than their attacker, but because they could not find the trigger. I believe that understanding how common attacks develop and the way people act to being confronted, is where your self protection starts. When and if things do get physical the hardest part is knowing when you are committed and how to trigger that all-important first strike.

If we take a look at the dictionary definition of trigger:

1/ a movable device for releasing a spring or catch and so setting off a mechanism (esp. that of a gun).
2/ an event, occurrence, etc., that sets off a chain reaction.
3/ set (an action or process) in motion; initiate, precipitate.
4/ fire (a gun) by the use of a trigger

If we take away the term "gun" and replace it with "head butt", "punch", "kick" or "finger strike to the eyes" we are still looking for the same mechanism. But instead of metal, gunpowder and lead we replace them with muscle, tendons and bone. And like the important parts of a gun that work to make the bullet fly to its target, if one of them is out of place nothing will happen. Because all the parts of the gun only work one way once the trigger is pulled the chain reaction is set and the rest is automatic. But the overwhelming choice is made by the finger that pulls the trigger, without being trigger happy a very important decision has to be made and at a time when you are under a lot of pressure.

If we don't give ourselves a point at which we can automatically by pass the minefield of fears we have about a confrontation, then our fears will take hold and freeze us to the spot. With awareness training we can see a potential attacker and if it's too late to avoid the confrontation we can still hold it off (just for a few seconds) with a defensive guard. But many fall victim to the waiting game hoping that things will get better and the confrontation will melt away.

It is not easy to decide that now is the time to fight. Decision making is the last thing your brain wants to do at this point, every technique you have ever fantasised about performing in a real fight just disappears. You need a trigger to pull, so your punch or kick is set in motion giving your muscles and tendons the same automatic release as the firing mechanism of a gun. This is not an impossible task. Training a simple response to fire at the sign of danger is like hitting the brakes in your car. If someone suddenly pulled out in front of you, you don't have to look for the middle pedal your foot automatically finds it. A trigger that is practised hundreds of times a week by millions of motorists throughout the country. At the end of the day a kick is a kick and a punch is a punch. Whatever you feel is your best form of attack should be the one you work to train your trigger response with.

Take The Thinking Out And Eliminate Doubt.

If you work on a punch bag you should not just do rounds of punching and kicking, this will build your power, speed and stamina but not a cold start trigger response. The following ideas should not replace but be added to your normal training programme.

1. Face the bag stand in fighting range say with your face 18 inches away from the bag. Now just throw from a cold start hard punches at the bag. After each punch relax your hands and drop them down to your side, work at about 10 hits per minute.

2. Face the bag in a short 45-degree stance. This time let your leading hand move up to touch the bag. As soon as your leading hand makes contact with the bag throw a rear hand punch. The touch of the lead hand is working as a touch trigger to fire the big punch, as before work at about 10 hits per minute and relax after each punch.

We are now building up an automatic response to the threat picked up by your lead hand. In a short time the touch of the lead hand triggering the rear hand becomes one and feels comfortable. What we are looking for is to build up muscle memory, we are teaching our muscles and our brain to do something without us having to think about who, where and when. Look at it this way. If you moved the coffee jar in your kitchen to a different cupboard for the

next few mornings when looking to make yourself a cup of coffee you will find yourself reaching into the wrong cupboard. You moved the jar, you know that it is in a new location, but for years your hand has reached for the same cupboard every morning. It's muscle memory that is taking you to the wrong cupboard.

The touch will control

And trigger your attack

It goes without saying that in our day to day lives we do find ourselves in close proximity to other people. And it would be over the top to punch everyone's lights out on the 5.45 from Waterloo just because they made contact with your leading hand. We are talking about a situation that you feel is a threat to your personal safety. The trigger helps you override the doubt and gives you a predetermined level at which you feel justified to respond to.

The touch trigger can work on many levels and it is personal to you. Our size, shape, sex and personal background will all add colour to the way in which we will control and operate a touch trigger. Again we come back to body language, within any group of people we have a complex unspoken language going on.

Verbal Triggers

A verbal trigger gives the same response as the touch trigger. But this time a particular word or phrase triggers your attack. Yes I know I used the phrase attack, why? Because that is the mind set you should be in to deal with someone that you perceive to be a threat. If you feel that you must wait for the other person to attack you first before you can enter a physical encounter, please come out from under that ignorance blanket you have pulled over your head.

If someone is standing in front of you pointing and verbally describing the beating they are about to give you, they have already started the race and if you do not act quickly you will find yourself on the floor still waiting for the sound of the starting pistol. This is a race that can be lost in seconds. They have already started their attack, from a pointing finger to a "What The Fuck You Looking AT". They have started their attack and are just waiting for their moment to strike.

One of the most common verbal triggers would be for your attacker to say, *"Its ok mate I don't want any trouble,"* They throw their punch on the T of trouble. Because they have done it before they know it works, as soon as they say the word their body reacts to the verbal trigger. Just like any form of training the more you get used to the technique the more it becomes natural. It is a sad fact that the majority of confrontations start with something many of us do not practise, verbal fighting technique. If you train with verbal triggers it helps you read the signs of someone setting you up for an attack. Someone who wishes to attack you will use dialogue to help them move in taking your mind off the threat.

This could be in the form of them asking you a question. *"Do you have the time? Do you have you change for the parking meter?"* Anything can be used. As you are being distracted by the question you are open to attack from the person asking the question or his mate coming up behind you. It may be a bit upsetting to think about how people will use this type of game plan. Forget upsetting they do it because it works. With this game plan they can take you out of the picture before you are able to even think about fighting back.

If they were being out and out aggressive you would be more on your guard. They don't want this, they want an easy victim. Saying anything to get you to go with them or keep you unaware of the danger. Remember body language, if they use a disarming appearance along with a soft-spoken tone of voice your mind set will not think of the danger you are in. You have to practise the approach of an attacker to help you understand how quickly you can become a victim. I know that people will use verbal aggression to pick on and breakdown a victim and we will look at that a bit later.

Talking to the pads

Striking on the trigger word

Let's talk

Because of the effects of adrenalin most of us will not be able to hold an in-depth conversation with someone who we feel is about to attack us. So we should practise using all the muscles in our body when it comes to looking to protect ourselves, and that includes the ones in the throat. From all your awareness training you will see the danger in time and get away.

Your voice is something adrenaline can take away from you when you feel under threat. So it's important to train your voice as with any other part of your training. If you come over positive this will go along away to help you in a situation. We want to be able to use the same game plan against our attacker. So like the muscle memory with touch trigger we train our voice to use certain phrases that can help us keep control of the situation or trigger our attack.

Lets look at a phrase that can work to help you get control or trigger your attack. *"Yes, can I help you"? "Sorry I don't know" "Can I help?"* is an open phrase. If you like, it can cover many questions or the fact that someone has stepped in too close to you and you wish them to move back. So you are controlling the distance between you and the person asking the question. Because you practise the phrase it can be used automatically. Again we are dealing with a situation that we feel uncomfortable with and feel the danger of us being attacked is great. So using the same phrase again, let's pick out a trigger word that could be used to start your attack.

"Yes can I help? **Sorry** *I don't know"* So we can use the word *"sorry"* to trigger our attack. Let's look at how we can train muscle memory to work from that trigger word.

1. Face your target (punch bag or focus mitts) don't just throw a punch. Wait. Talk out loud to the target. When you say **sorry** within the context of a sentence throw your big punch. After every strike relax your hands down by your side and repeat.

2. This time work the touch with the verbal trigger. By using the lead hand to touch the target, switch between the two triggers to launch your attack.

As an Instructor I have found that the hardest part of doing the above drills is the embarrassment most people feel in talking out loud to a bag. Like anything new, in time the embarrassment disappears because you soon realise how important it is to understand and practise how people will attack in the street. As I said before this is not to replace but to be added to your normal training program. All of my students have found it a great boost to their understanding of how to make what they know work for real and under pressure. And many have gone on to have deep and meaningful relationships with their punch bags or focus mitts?

Chapter 7

THE FENCE

If you want to protect something from damage it's a good rule of thumb to keep it in a safe place. If you did have to move it, you would place it in a box with lots of packing material. If you want to protect your home from unwelcome visitors good strong doors and window locks (as long as you remember to close and lock them) will keep out the opportunist burglar. With garden gates, intruder floodlights, burglar alarm and a big dog you will put off the majority of burglars.

So with the house you are building bigger and bigger fences for the burglar to climb before he can get his hands on your property. So it makes sense to think of ourselves as needing some form of alarm to protect us as we go about a normal routine. A portable high wall we could carry with us at all times would be a good idea, something an attacker would have to climb over before he could get his hands on us. Colour codes and awareness techniques will cover a great distance and will give you lots of warning of danger, but the fence is the front door and you keep it closed.

So how can we make it work.

Every one of us enjoys our own personal space and we all feel uncomfortable if someone without our consent enters that space. This is our space, this is our front room, kitchen and bedroom. PRIVATE KEEP OUT Only people we know and trust can come in. In fact we all manipulate this range every day from taking the train into work where our personal space is bumped pushed and shoved all the way into work. Negotiating our way around the super market where the shopping trolley becomes an extension to our space, as we move up and down the aisle looking for the milk. When we have to move out the way because some ignorant pig has left his trolley in the middle of the aisle and has nipped off to the other side to pick up another cut-price loaf. Now he's walking backwards head high to see what's on the top shelf. With the front of his trolley now swinging from side to side as if it was a medieval ball and chain. But you keep all the frustration to yourself, through half closed eyes you whisper to yourself "what an ignorant pig". But when his shopping trolley makes contact with your trolley you know its war.

Apart from the fact that I am not a happy shopper, what can we learn from the shopping trolley example? We can all move our personal space not just distance but into objects. Not convinced? How about not letting a fellow motorist into your lane in heavy traffic. Not only is your car your personal space but you now feel the 2 or 3 metres in front of you is as well. So we have this built in radar working all the time, pinging away telling us if someone is within our personal space. It is up to us how we respond. If it is a social occasion and someone is too close we may just take a step back or sit back in our seat. We have not built a brick wall just a little more space, but we all understand the signs of social etiquette and it may as well be a six-foot wall. So the fence does not have to be a physical one, but what if the person doesn't take any notice and wants to try the front door, so to speak. The physical fence can be used to check your distance and most of us do it all the time when we talk to each other. Your hands move to describe the size of a fish you caught once or how someone overtook you on the motorway.

Using our hands to describe events, the shape or pointing out relevant parts of a conversation. Imagine you are at a party and you're telling a funny story to some friends and like all good parties everyone is crammed in the kitchen, when someone carrying a load of drinks wants to get through.

Your group will carry on with the story and at the same time move to let the person through. There is not enough room to stroke a cat let alone swing one. But everyone in the group makes room to let the person through, they close in on each other's personal space to let the stranger through. They may even put their hands out to guide the person through, with all this going on they are still able to enjoy the funny story. When the person is out of the way everyone moves back to their personal space, some would have used a physical fence to guide the person through but all would have moved their personal space. Now imagine that the person carrying all the drinks trips as he is making his way through, all the drinks are sent flying. This time there is danger from the flying glass. The group will cut out the funny story, change their personal space and all put up a physical fence to protect themselves from the glasses flying in the air.

So a physical fence is something we do all the time every day 24-7. In our sleep we are controlling our space. Even my 5-year-old daughter can do it. If at 4o'clock in the morning she decides to climb into bed with mum and dad the space she can clear will have dad sleeping the rest of the night on the sofa. The amount of information we can take in and give through our fingertips is amazing. From the comfort of someone putting a caring hand on our shoulder to the threat felt by someone poking a finger into our chest.

We can see danger coming from a long way off or hearing the sound of breaking glass, which will have us looking to see what the problem was. The sound of glass breaking has triggered a response to duck down or see if the threat is coming for us. If you have ever been in a pub packed with people, the noise from the jukebox and people having a good time could be deafening. If someone behind the bar drops a glass the sound cuts across everything in the pub. People will stop talking and look, some people to break the feeling of fear, which comes from associating broken glass with danger, and will then jeer at the bar staff in relief.

So being aware of our surrounding is a long distance guard and keeping the threat of danger as far away as possible. Some things from a loud noise in the street to the slight squeak of someone down stairs opening a door if we are tucked up in bed will bring on the sense of danger. And we will want to back away, the sudden noise may make us jump and the noise down stairs may have you covering up under the blankets. Whatever it is you'll want you put something between you and the threat, distance or a shield.

So the idea of putting up a guard or fence is something we can all do, and to some degree we all have an understanding of how we control our space by using our hands. Like the idea of being in the kitchen at a party, we can see that the physical fence is done at very close range. This is the range that physical attacks take place in so it's an important part of the picture and one you must understand if you are going to protect yourself. Still giving you the choice to control the situation, to make your escape or using dialogue along with your touch trigger to use your pre-emptive strike.

Building a fence

Lets start by being in a relaxed standing position with your hands by your side. Now slowly bring your hands up and in front of you. Stop when your elbows are just above your waist and with your hands open and your palms facing up. With your fingertips just inside your personal space try this out with a friend or just stand close to a wall, this is a non-aggressive fence. You are in control of your space and you may find yourself doing this type of hand movement when you are talking to people. Think about the last time you described to a friend that you found this great new shop. As you tell your friend you go down the high street your hand will move forward and when you get to the baker's shop you turn right, now your fingers get in on the act and start pointing right. If you have any friends that enjoy fishing at the weekends you will already be familiar with just how much someone can exaggerate their personal space by describing the size of the fish that got away.

Practice talking with a fence

Non-aggressive Fence

This would be with opened handed movements moving in and out controlling the distance between you and the attacker. Showing your hands open will make you seem non-aggressive, but keeping you in control of the situation before you feel the threat is so great that you need to pre-empt their attack.

Using dialogue to talk the person down from the situation or using it to distract them before you strike by using a touch or verbal trigger.

The fence is not static. Keeping it moving is a way of relieving the stress of the situation. But something to bear in mind when you practise it, is try and have the level at which you hold your hands when you strike always the same. When I use the opened hand fence my lead hand will be at a height that is level with my attacker's chest. Because the distance between most people's chests and their jaw line is the length of my palm to my fingertips on my lead hand. So when I train my strike on the punch bag by touching the bag with my lead hand, my rear hand be it a palm strike or right hook will know where the target is without looking for it.

So we're back to muscle memory. If you repeat it over and over you will do it without thinking. Try this little trick; clap your hands together, well done. Easy yes? Now clap to your left side, now to your right side, behind you and above your head, do it again with your eyes closed. How many times did you miss? None? Told you it was easy, because we have learnt to know where our hands are from the moment we are born. As babies to pick up things and bring them to our mouths and as toddlers finding the flap on the video can be opened with one hand and a chocolate biscuit can be pushed in with the other. So we can train a gap into the equation. Still not with me on this? What about when you sit behind the steering wheel of a car your left hand on the wheel your right hand puts the key in the ignition. That's training a gap, no matter what it is something repeated will be set in your muscle memory. From starting a car to tightening your shoelace the same memory can be used to land your first strike. Ok back to the fence. Your lead hand is acting like a short range radar every time the person in front of you moves in you feel the ping of the radar and keep your personal distance in control.

As you talk you can stay switched on to what the person is doing and staying in control. You set the limit to how many times you let the person touch your fence before you attack, but if they are moving in after the first touch don't wait too long.

Aggressive Fence

First buy a big dog and I mean the biggest and most vicious dog you can get, shave your head and have "kill" tattooed across your forehead, throw in some boots, braces and a white tee shirt and you will have a good aggressive fence.

Get the idea? Its giving people the impression that you are the hardest thing on the planet and if they pick on you then they are in deep shit. Inside you may be as hard as dribbling slug and one grain of salt will have you melt away. But your outward appearance is a fence most will not want to climb over. Aggression is the fence most of us would have seen at sometime. Someone switching on your fear of how dangerous you believe this person to be. Most times it's a mind game, people bluffing each other, pushing and shoving, shouting and pointing with neither wanting to make the first move because each fears the other. People doing this are at a stalemate with the edge of each other's fence touching the other. One will make the first move and attack, or one of them will back down by moving away but still verbally attacking the other.

So if you wish to use an aggressive fence then you make yourself appear a real threat. Shouting, making threats that if they want to fight you then you are going to

Training controlling Distance and Threat

eat them alive. It can work very well, if you can make yourself look and sound like a nutter people tend to back off. But be careful, if you don't understand how the aggression game is played and your bluff is called then you will be fighting without the advantage of the pre-emptive attack. You will be fighting in the deep end. You could try and switch it around and go back to being non-aggressive to try and set them up again. But this situation is going on too long, if someone is using an aggressive fence and is staying back from your personal space most times it's for show. Using the person's fear of them to win the confrontation without fighting.

Putting the triggers with the fence

Like I said before the trigger can be verbal or physical by working them with the fence you can train them together and find the one that works best for you.

Practice outside – It will make a difference

When you work with the physical trigger remember this is not letting your attacker throw the first punch. It could be them just poking you in the chest or your lead hand making contact with them. Again the time scale we are talking about here is very small from their first threat to their attack, say 10 seconds. So you can see that your strike will be more effective as a triggered reflex rather than a last minute battle plan. Try it out on a punch bag, touch the bag with the lead hand from your fence, on the second or third touch strike the bag. This is building your automatic triggered reflex attack. After training it a few hundred times you will find your muscles that you use for the striking will work without you having to think about it. The muscles in your body remember what to do because you have trained your triggered attack so many times. So no more mental logjam about what you are going to use to fight back with, you just do it.

With the verbal trigger, it's the same as the touch but this time you can hold them off with the fence and attack them when you use your particular word or phrase to trigger your attack. The good thing about this is that it gets you to practise talking at a time when it is normally the last thing on your mind. So you come across as more confident. If you are not sure about this idea, I have seen many people (myself included) attacked in mid sentence. Believe me, it works.

So being able to talk within a dangerous situation is important. Giving you time to get to grips with the situation. And as your voice has the ability to disappear when you find yourself confronted, so when you train your fence and attack triggers always practise talking to the attacker/punch bag.

I know it may sound a strange thing to do but your voice is a fence and a very valuable tool to get that winning edge. Most of us have talked to ourselves at some time and moaned about something that's gone wrong at home or at work. I sure you have all played the hero in your head and looked at yourself in the mirror. "You talking to me? Well I'm the only one here; you must be talking to me," BANG! Ring any bells?

CHAPTER 8

Be pre-emptive and prevent the bigger problem

I have been talking a lot about being pre-emptive with your attack and I have referred to how the physical side to protecting yourself is a small part of the picture. The pre-emptive strike is the basis of self protection when all other avenues have not been successful. Walking away, not getting out of your car, leaving the pub because someone or something has made you feel uncomfortable. But when the threat will not back off and all the signs are telling you that it is about to kick off, you must be first with your physical attack.

This may well be the hardest thing for you to do at the time and it is never easy no matter what you may think. But your mindset should be locked into always looking to avoid a situation, but mentally prepared to attack when you have no other option. For me to say *"attack your attacker before they have made any physical contact with you",* for a lot of people is something they find hard to take on board. Also the fact that dealing with someone who at first sight may not appear to be a problem, because they look ok has nothing to do with what someone is capable of. And why I have been going on about awareness at all times. You should always be on the lookout and ready to take any action that will get you out of trouble.

Imagine that you were walking up to a cliff, *"Got myself a crying, walking, sleeping, talking, living doll",* well maybe, but a cliff with a couple of hundred feet drop, with rocks and crashing sea at the bottom would be more scary. Now you will have no problem as you are walking up to the edge with the safety of solid earth under your feet. As you get closer to the edge you begin to slow down because you know the danger ahead and the fall that awaits you if you carry on walking. You are pre-empting the danger by slowing down and preventing the bigger problem of falling off the cliff. So doing something before you lose the chance to alter the outcome makes sense. If you stopped on the edge of the cliff and waited you could slip you can now only be sure of one thing, you are going to hit the rocks at the bottom. You could die, lose a leg, break your back on the rocks or drown as the high tide covers you and the rocks. All this pain, because you stayed too long on the edge of the cliff.

If you stood on the edge and found yourself falling forward you would throw yourself back. Your instinct to survive overriding any fascination you may have about being on the edge. So instinct can take over and get you to do something, be it jump back to safety or if you are falling putting your hands forward to brake your fall. Which is ok if you trip on the pavement, but is as good as shit on a stick, if you are going to plunge hundreds of feet onto rocks.

PRE-EMPTIVE STRIKE

You have the right to protect yourself. You do not have to wait for the person to grab hold or hit you first. If you do not make the first strike you are fighting off the back foot and will soon be on the floor. If your mindset is to wait for them to attack first, your options for getting away, with as little damage done to yourself will be greatly diminished.

As I am writing I have just had a phone call form a friend of mine Liz Clark who is a registered self-defence instructor. She has just told me about how people are being attacked by people posing as perfume sellers. Walking up to women asking them if they would like to try this perfume. As the women go to smell the perfume they are sprayed with something that incapacitates them. They are then robbed. Talk about waiting to be attacked or blocking then countering an attacker. How the hell would you do that with a face full of gas?

If a government goes to war a pre-emptive action can be seen as necessary to win the battle and save the lives of thousands, may be millions. If a military action can be seen as intending to prevent attack by disabling the enemy (a pre-emptive strike) with all the back up, men, arms, and money a government has at its disposal and they would still fight on a pre-emptive basis. So if you want to have a strategy you know works and has been proven in war, countless battles throughout the ages and is beating people everyday in street confrontation; if you fear for your safety then that strategy is pre-empting their attack. You may feel that war and street crime can't be seen in the same way, well they can because people die in both.

What's a fair fight?

God may know the answer to this one. But as someone once said, *"How the hell can a priest bless soldiers going into battle to kill other human beings".* So man will interpret a law, human or holy. Whatever way you look at it something bad comes out of fighting that's for sure. People get kill or scarred for life, family and friends feel the pain of loss or feel the stress and worrying over a hurt loved one.

So if there is a strong down side to fighting what's a fair fight? Look out because I'm sending this question back into your court. If you feel its right to fight over everything then there is not much I can say that will change your mind. If you feel that part of a good night out is to kick shit out of someone because it rounds off an evening's entertainment before you go for a curry, then I'm talking to a wall. And the type of person that anyone of us maybe faced with; someone who just wants to kick off over anything. They enjoy the feeling, the buzz, the fact you the victim could be the nicest person on this planet means nothing you are just an easy victim. The cry of, *"What about that night we kicked the guy so many times he looked like a pizza"* becomes the starting blocks to another race to find a victim, with each story of the previous night's victory fuelling the fire.
With people like this on the lookout for trouble the word fair is not found in their vocabulary. So I'm talking to you the reader, a normal person. Someone who wants to move up and move on in

life and who has moved up the evolutionary links and no longer drags their knuckles along the ground.

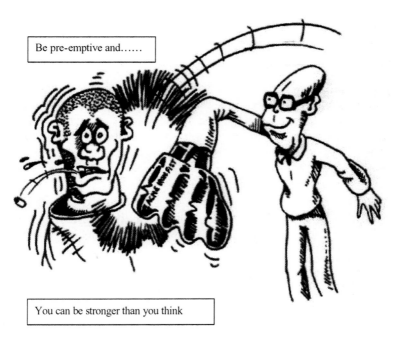

In the full knowledge that I am repeating myself again, avoid situations as soon as you become aware of them. Work hard at understanding the signals that warn you of danger, and have a game play ready to put into action as soon as you feel under threat or find yourself in a dangerous situation. At the beginning of the book I talked about how dealing with your awareness, fears and consequences are the greatest and hardest things to come to terms with when looking to defend yourself. I hope you have been switched onto the points I have been making. If you have identified yourself with some of the feelings and worries to do with confrontations I have talked about in this book, then you are someone who like almost everyone else that makes up the population is a normal modern human being. And just like most of us, trying to understand the beauty and the brutality of the world we live in, and at the same time trying to make the best of the short time we all have left.

I also said that we will look at the kicking and punching bit to fighting back later, well we are not there yet, just a couple more ideas to run past you first. But as to being first with your physical defence it must be looked at as the golden rule. Pre-emptive attacks are a way to win against someone who maybe bigger and stronger than you. Or you may be out numbered with 2 or more attackers confronting you, striking first gives you the leading edge in a street fight. If you wait for the person to instigate the attack with a punch or a kick, your counter will not be effective. Taking one of the attackers out first gives you the advantage and the opportunity to get away.

You could train for 10 years in something but if someone kicks off before you, by knocking you out with a punch, glassing you in the face or shoving a meat skewer in your eye, you are out of the picture. You can take your physical training as far as you like and train in as many different fighting systems as you can get your hands on. But no matter who or how many people you train with, make whatever they give you valuable. Remember you are the one who has to make it work under the high pressure of real violence.

Be switched on all the time. When you feel under threat and you fear the person is about to attack, be pre-emptive, you attack first.

How are we doing for coffee and biscuits? Put the book down and refuel.

Chapter 9

The Law

He turns to see his friend falling, the sound of broken glass cutting the air. Unable to move everything around him seemed to slow down, the sight of his friend covered in blood is clear, but everything else is a blur.

In the few seconds it has taken you to read the above and with the brutal scenario flashing through your mind, how would you interpret any legal points to what has just happen or what would be your course of action? To list the legal points would take a book, in fact hundreds of books. Bookshelves in solicitor's offices throughout the land groan under the weight of legal terminology. It is always easier to judge a situation in hindsight. But you may have less time than it took you to read the opening lines in this chapter to make a life or death decision. What would you do?

Throughout this book I have put across the fact that protecting yourself is all about controlling any situation you find yourself in. The physical part is small and in most cases unnecessary, but when it does get physical where do we stand? There are some basic points you should understand about your rights but above all your private rights as person come first.

Section 3(1) of the Criminal Law Act 1967 states: *'A person may use such force as is reasonable in the circumstances, in the prevention of a crime, or in effecting or assisting in the lawful arrest of offenders or suspected persons unlawfully at large.'*

It goes without saying that your rights change from country to country but your basic human right is to protect yourself. Yes you should have an understanding of the law to support your actions, but it should never interfere with you dealing with a situation at the time. I am not putting forward the Sex Pistols view of Anarchy in the UK. Nor am I for one minute saying we should arm ourselves to the teeth and shoot the person in front of us at the supermarket checkout, just because they are writing a cheque for a pint of milk. It's ok having the information about your legal rights. But one thing is for sure, if someone has decided to attack you, then he has thrown your rights out of the window. Your rights at the time of being attacked, raped or abducted are what your attacker is willing to give you. And as I keep saying you fight back when you are in fear for your safety, not over who parked their car in your space.

As much as the law gives you the right to protect yourself it is our personal fears of any possible legal backlash that can make you hesitate. The personal baggage it makes you carry can slow you down when it comes to protecting yourself. It is the one question people always ask me when I'm teaching and the one that most people have the greatest fear of. Sometimes more than being hurt themselves. You can find yourself fixated by the legal consequences and all feed your personal fear of ending up in prison for protecting yourself.

"My good man, please try and understand I have the law on my side"

I am not going to go into every legal right you have or what you can or cannot do. Why? Because having all the information in the world to your legal rights will not help you when someone has picked you out as a victim. If you believe that someone is going to attack you and you are in fear of legal comebacks, you could die waiting.

You have the legal right to strike the first blow if you genuinely fear for your safety. And like I have been saying you are not picking fights, your main interest is avoiding them.

The law says that a person charged with a crime may plead that he acted as he did to protect himself, or his property or others from attack, or to prevent a crime. This, strictly speaking, is not a "defence", but a justification for the conduct, which, if successfully pleaded, makes the conduct lawful.

It is clear that a person may make a pre-emptive strike. *'A man about to be attacked,'* said Lord Griffith in one case, *'does not have to wait for the assailant to strike the first blow or fire the first shot.'* Neither does he, or she, have to retreat before using force. The force must be 'necessary' but it is left to juries to decide if an assailant could have been avoided rather than attacked.

If you can see the situation developing then your first reaction must be to get away beforehand. If you are unable to and you have to strike first then your actions are easy to justify. With the main justification being made to yourself, because you are the one face-to-face and dealing with it. Justify your actions to the police if they come knocking on your door or to the judge or the 12 people on the jury. You can plead your case afterwards in the courts if needs must, but you can never plead your case from a box, which is six feet under.

What's reasonable in the circumstances when its all gone wrong?

Your right is to strike first when you honestly believe you are about to be attacked. Being able to pull off a pre-emptive strike can end the confrontation quickly. Some of you may be thinking that its ok if I can pull off a first strike one shot knock out and be on my toes before my attacker comes round. But what if I can't hit first or it goes wrong and I'm dragged into an alleyway or taken off in a car. I'm in fear for my life. How far can I go to get away from the situation?

Let's look at it like this. You may have been unable to strike the first blow. For whatever reason something went wrong and you find you are being dragged, kicked and beaten. What level of threat to your safety say on a scale of 1-10 do you think this situation would put you in?

Yes you are in the deep end, you are in no doubt about the situation now. It would be reasonable to say you are in deep shit. Reason has gone from the situation; you can't set limits until you are safe and no longer in danger. Say in grabbing your attacker you find you can reach his face and can push your fingers into his eyes. He screams in pain and releases his hold on you and you get away. Would you think your defence was reasonable? What if he lost his sight in one eye would you feel that your defence was reasonable? Would your actions have been reasonable in the circumstances?

This reasonable question has to be seen as what you consider reasonable at the time of the threat or attack. And as long as your response to the threat or attack takes place at the same time, you could argue how reasonable you have been. It's your perception of the danger you are in at the time that counts to what you did to defend yourself as being reasonable. If you end up in court with your now one eyed attacker outraged at having lost a eye, it may be difficult for the jury to judge your action in a calm court room. They were not at the scene; they did not feel your fear and they were not taking part in the nightmare you found yourself in.

Lord Morris *'a person cannot wait to a nicety the exact measure of his necessary defensive action'.*

With every thing that is going on around you, your judgement as to how dangerous the situation is will be instinctive. At that point in time you are fighting for your life. So in a hands on battle you remove your attacker's eye and this stops the attack on you. Then you could argue your defence was reasonable at the time. But after getting the attacker off you, you left the scene and as you turn the street corner you found a piece of lead pipe in the road. It would not be reasonable for you to walk back to the scene and begin to beat him with the pipe or your hands for that matter. Your concern is to get away, if you need medical help get to the hospital or telephone the emergency services.

Stay out of the minefield

I have no doubt that when it comes to people dealing with the minefield of what, how and when, to the law question, it's a fact that many will beat themselves into submission by fearing the legal outcome. The fact is that your attacker could not give a dam or has been down this legal road before. They may know what to say to the police and will have you standing in the minefield. The fact that some people will attack, stab, rob, rape and kill is a measure of the type and times we live in. Also the number of times many innocent victims fall foul to the law as well adds more insult to injury.

I do believe that you should do everything in your power to say away from trouble. But in the real world sometime trouble knocks on your door without warning. And it is hard to stay reasonable in the circumstances; I sure most people if they found a burglar in their house would love to get their hands on them. Pulling the burglar back through an open window and slamming them into the floor then holding them until the police arrive would be great. I mean you caught him red handed. But could you resist the feeling of wanting to kick his testicles so hard you turned them into something that resembles pork mince.

Thank god that the majority of people are only interested in enjoying life. What with work and paying bills most of us have little time to do this. The last thing we need is to worry about how far can I legally go to stop this person from killing me. Most of us take care to look after our personal belongings from locking the car to home security. If we did a little bit more about avoiding and preparing for confrontations we could reduce the risk.

As a society we need rules and laws to help the millions of us to go about our daily lives. We may moan about some of them from time to time and some laws may be wrong or seen as unjust and slow. But on the whole your rights as a citizen work. But it only takes one person to enter your life just for a few seconds that can take your rights and life away.

A personal view

Information is power. Knowing your rights when it comes to protecting yourself is helpful, but only if you can survive the attack to quote them.

I am not a violent man; I have many good and some bad points, which I am sure my wife will remind me of after reading this book. I get on with most people and the ones that do piss me off I make sure I have little or no contact with. I will mostly walk away from situations that I do not feel comfortable with, but I will step in and help anyone I feel needs it.
I consider myself a helpful and law abiding person. But I will protect my family and loved ones and if forced to, I will use any means and do anything to win.

Chapter 10

Aggression Frustration and Deception

Being confronted by what we perceive to be overwhelming odds can, with the right attitude and understanding give us the winning edge. All of us feel and can relate to a situation that would make us feel angry and also a time when we have felt afraid.

Remember it is how we interpret what we feel that can make the feeling get worse. Adrenalin without doubt has the greatest affect on us, giving or taking away our ability to perform in a dangerous confrontation. The adrenalin release is the same as if we were about to step off the edge of a high diving board, or take on the challenge of a theme park roller coaster ride. The fear response is the same; it is how we interpret the feeling. So the screams of excitement on the roller coaster can turn itself into fear and panic on the street when face to face with a street confrontation. It is our perception of the release of adrenalin that makes us feel enjoyment or fearful. Yes I know I'm repeating myself, but the difference is between shitting yourself or handling it.

Regular exposure to the effects gives you an understanding of what is going on inside you and how your body will react. But you need to have a benchmark to work from, because it's your body's response to release adrenalin whether you want it to or not. Understanding your level and being able to control it before you hit the panic button is vital. Exposure helps you to become more familiar with how your body feels under pressure. Recognising and understanding adrenalin helps you to control the feeling.

Get into the pool

If you want to learn to swim, at some point you have to get into the water and get wet. For most of us this is done step by step from baby pool with armbands to floats and kicking from the side of the pool. Then in time we build up the confidence to push off from the side and swim our first length. But from the day we started learning to swim we are in the water feeling unsafe with the fear of the water all around us, but with the safety of armbands floats and a warm indoor pool we can handle the feeling.

So imagine yourself just being told the basic principals of swimming (hold your breath, rotate arms and kick your legs) then being pushed off the side of a ship into the middle of the North Sea. Do you think you would panic just a little bit, or do you think you would fill your 'Y' fronts and die?

Whenever we think about swimming, the idea of not being in the water never comes in to the equation. You learn to cope with the fear of the water and mechanical skills of swimming all at the same time. So you can look at aggression and fear training as the water in the pool, you have to find out if your technical information can work for you in the water. And just like your first step into the baby pool you do it one step at a time. You don't want to find yourself falling in the deep end without first knowing what it feels like to get wet.

Anger can take the pain away

I have punched through a lath and plaster wall breaking some knuckles in my hand and ripping the skin to the bone, no pain. Kicked a dinning room table so hard the top flipped in the air ripping out the bolted on legs, no pain. The hand got better and after a stay in hospital and 14 stitches later so did my leg, for days after the injuries hurt but at the time of anger and aggression no pain. So the up side to fear and aggression is the adrenalin that kicks in will also give you your own personal supply of pain relief. The pain relief could be your armbands or float in a real confrontation, giving you that edge to fight or to get away from greater danger.

The shock of an aggressive attack for many will end most street fights, but it can also switch on a great power inside you when it's in your face. If you train to protect yourself in the street you should understand a strong verbal attack is just as powerful as a good right hook. Most street fights are won or lost by the verbal attack, your adrenalin kicks in, and your fear breaks you down without a punch being thrown. In a violent confrontation your body will be screaming at you to run when your attacker is so close his breath is making your eyes water. You are blind in the swimming pool without a float and the girls from Baywatch are not going to dive in to save you.

You are stronger than you think, remember it's how you interpret your feelings. If you've never had the chance to understand and feel the feelings before in your training, you've been swimming without getting wet.

The intricate movements many will put into a defensive technique or control and takedown with a training partner always amaze me. Because when they try to

Make sure your partner can put you under pressure

do the same thing under pressure it doesn't work, they believe they need to train more on their technique. It's not understanding that it is the pressure of the situation that is letting them down. Like a pressure cooker that cooks your dinner in double quick time because of the intense heat, without a pressure release valve of understanding the situation, you will be cooked in double quick time.

The Frustration of holding back

Most of us have to control the pressure valve of frustration at some point everyday, you may have forgotten to set the video and missed the last programme in the series. Or found yourself waiting at the end of a queue only to find the thing you wanted to buy has sold out. No milk in the morning, no toilet paper (should have checked before you started). The angry customer who has been shouting in your face for 15 min about the clock they bought from this shop and that does not work. At which point you would love to hit them in the face with the musical clock that plays *"Pack up your troubles in your old kitbag and smile, boys smile"* on the hour. But you don't. It's one more frustration that you hold in. In fact frustrations throughout the day can just keep adding up and because we have to keep a lid on that pressure cooker it can take its toll.

This can just keep building from the start of the day. First having to use that page from the newspaper to wipe your backside on. Then missing the train into work and being told off by the boss because you were late. Now this customer's clock that has stopped working after two years, to which you find the reason why, is because the customer has not changed the batteries. So you change the batteries free of charge just to keep the peace, and on walking out of the shop the customer does not even say "thank you". The frustrations just add up.

Most of us have this type of thing happen to us everyday, the pressure builds up inside us until we can release it. Now this could be in the gym or for some people it comes out as aggression. Towards the people they meet on their way home from work, may be in the form of road rage. Or the person copes with the frustration staying in a high stress level all week and releasing it all on a Friday night with a belly full of beer. Now we all deal with problems in our own way but the point that I want to get across is your frustration and aggression feed each other. You can be strong and determined with them and if you know how they feel you can control them and use them at the right time. If you need to fight back at sometime you will be fighting with a mass of feelings not just aggression or frustration.

Speaking for myself I have to let day-to-day stress out. I do this by hitting my punch bag, playing music in the car or just sitting down and taking control until I can let it out. I can normally feel the build up depending on the type of day I've had. But when the pressure builds to high it comes out as raw aggression. It will not be aimed at the people around me but if I can't release it on the punch bag, then a cupboard door or kitchen worktop will do. In one house my wife and I had there was a cupboard under the stairs with a solid wood door. It must have been well made because it stood up to many a good beating. I don't hit my wife or my kids the point is I feel the build up and control the release. But I have lost count of the people I have stopped myself from decking because I've been able to control the feeling. Ok I have been honest about how I release the aggression; ok about the wife look

Everyday we are faced with problems in which we have to hold our frustrations

3.00AM

between you and me if I ever raised a hand to her she would beat the crap out of me.

You could think it's a bit of a pain having to replace doors, cupboards and worktops, but it's better than hitting the people you care for. I have found that by understanding, I can deal with it and in turn this goes a long way to controlling the aggression and using it when I have to. As I said before I feel I have a friendly personality. Ok the outside shell may well resemble a fat scary blob, but inside the person is ok. But I can explode into the role of a maniac by releasing my internal pressure cooker, which can help me take control of a situation and stop the threat in its tracks.

So a certain amount of aggression/frustration must stay inside me, and the weird thing is if I do have to release this at someone then the feeling can come from a long way back. People, places or things that happened years ago flash into my mind and I can use this to explode with my attack. So the anger I am putting into my attack may not come from the person in front of me, but from feelings I have had inside may be for years. Once I pull the trigger (so to speak) the bullets are armed with everything I can put in them. Because as I've talked about before, once the trigger is pulled the rest is automatic.

Another look at triggers

Where as before I talked about verbal and touch triggers another very workable trigger is with aggression. Like the physical trigger works when you make contact by touching the person with say your lead hand. If they do not stop coming forward the second touch triggers your pre-emptive strike. And with the verbal trigger you use your pre-emptive strike when you say your trigger word.

You train with verbal and touch triggers to build your automatic response to give you a reflex attack rather than trying to make plans at the last minute. You are playing a role using deception to keep your attacker off guard. Training the idea on a punch bag a few hundred times you find your muscles will make the strike without you having to think about them. The muscles in your body remember what to do because you have trained your pre-emptive strike so many times. So no more mental logjam about what technique you are going to use.

I have found by switching aggression I can show and tell the person that I'm going to be a nightmare to deal with. Remember the down side being that you can lose the shock of an unseen pre-emptive strike, but you will be fired up if it does kick off. This is in most cases a bluff, by showing raw aggression you can switch on your attacker's fear that you may be just a too big a problem.

Your size does not mean you are weak or strong. One night a friend of mine was walking home. She was switched on to the fact how dangerous walking alone as a woman can be. One night as the man walked past her she did not worry about it too much, because he did not come too close to her or say anything he just walked by. She was small, standing just over 5 foot with shoes on and weighing about 7stone. She found herself suddenly grabbed from behind and lifted of the ground and feeling absolutely terrified. And in her own words she said she went absolutely fucking crazy, shouting and fighting back as hard as she could.

This pretty young thing had turn into a pit bull, a kicking; scratching, wiggling devil she said it seemed to go on for a long time. But then the guy let go and just dropped her to the floor. She thought that he was about to attack again, but when she got up she saw he was running away. His target had turned into a nightmare. She did not know any of the fighting arts and had never been on a self-defence course. What she did do was to fight back on instinct and trigger her anger at her attacker.

Deception Attack with a smile

Understanding how attackers work will help you to see the problem and also let you turn the tables on them. Geoff Thompson put one of the most revealing insights to this forward as understanding the Four D's in his book Dead or Alive. Making the point that the four D's, dialogue, deception, distraction and destruction are techniques often used by particular attackers especially muggers and rapists.

Making the point that attacks can take place at anytime and it's not always a shouting match with two puffed out chests about to fight. Understanding the cold calm natural way someone can attack will help you protect against it. The four D's is a good insight in recognising an attacker's ploy, and I would like to thank Geoff for letting me use it in this book.

The Four D's

Dialogue - Dialogue designed to disarm and distract the potential victim are the most common first technique to be used. An attacker will approach the victim in a non-threatening way and begin a conversation.

This could be in the form of asking for directions, if you have the time, a light or spare change. Etc. His objective is to make you think about the question so that your attention is distracted from the weapon he is carrying or his accomplice coming up behind you.

Understanding his game plan will make you aware and keep alert.

Deception - An attacker will use deception to make himself appear harmless. His dialogue or his appearances are the most common methods that he uses to deceive his victim, and makes them let down their guard.

You cannot expect dangerous people to stand out in a crowd. Attackers may start with politeness or even with an ingratiating approach. Deception is the attacker's greatest asset.

Distraction - Is a part of deception and usually comes through dialogue. The attacker will ask the victim a question and then initiate the attack while the victim is probably thinking about the answer.

This distraction switches off any instinctive response the victim may have had; the victim is stripped of his ability to fight back by this simple ploy.

If the distraction is submissive, "I don't want any trouble, can we talk about it?" It will also take your assailant down from a state of fight or flight to one of low awareness.

Because your submissiveness tells him that the danger is over and he can relax into self-congratulation.

Brain engagement using the disarming/distracting dialogue gives the victim a "blind second", and this is when the assailant will strike.

An experienced attacker, to take down any protective fence that the victim may have constructed also uses distraction.

Destruction - This is the final part of the priming technique. Few people will come through the first physical blow; it will be over before most people realise that it had begun.

The attacker uses all the above to prime a victim that has only trained in a physical response.
Turning up the heat

The following ideas are just some of the ways I train with people to bring the real feeling of fear and aggression from the street, onto the training mat. We all have our own reasons for training along with the difference in age and sex. These drills may not be for everyone. Only you can tell if you are ready to give them a try, no one should be forced to try them. I'm just trying to get you to test the water and to give you a new perspective. One of the first drills I use to get the students to just feel uncomfortable is to stand face to face and very close. Being inside each other's comfort zone and looking into each other's eyes will bring on an uncomfortable feeling. To turn it up just a little bit one person could just push their partner away and as they step back the partner moves in and repeats the aggressive push.

Using the same drill again but this time as you push your partner away you add strong verbal aggression. Now you may not like or agree with the use of street language when you are training and I can understand that with children and with mixed ages and sexes in many classes. But you can still turn up the heat. Get wet in the shallow end of the pool and work your way to the deep end. So let's set the training drill pressure from 1-10.

Just shouting and pushing your partner would be 2 on this scale. Normal compliant training with a partner would be 0. You don't have to start F'ing & Blinding at each other build up to that. It's not always what you say but how you say it. You could shout cake, but if your face is full of anger and you did it with an aggressive posture, pointing or shaking a closed fist will get an effect. If you were on holiday in a different country and don't speak the language and someone confronted you, his body language and the tone of his voice would trigger your fear, understanding what the words mean doesn't come into it. In time and if your training partner is willing try adding the more colourful words. This will push the scale to a good 4. Remember this is not personal, but you will feel very uncomfortable and that's good as you are starting to get wet.

The good thing about these drills is they are safe, you are not in any danger because your partner is not going to hit you. But your body will feel fear because it is a primal reaction to which the only way not to feel it is not to take part. But with exposure to the feeling you can start to control and understand, to feel the feeling in safety is better than the blind shock of a street confrontation. The higher training levels do contain contact but you can build up to this in your own time, just keep adding that little bit more. In a short time you will find yourself feeling comfortable with the aggression drills, in fact you will be doing the drills more aggressively but you will feel much more in control. This is not the time to stop but to take it onto the next level. Now with the two partner drills you add being aggressive back with both of you pushing and verbally attacking. You both feel and switch on your own adrenalin rush. Now we are hitting 5 on the pressure scale.

The next two levels are harder and do involve impact as part of the drill. If you take the same level of aggression as level 5 but this time your partner holds a focus pad. Now as you explode your aggression, you hit the pad, but at the same time your partner can attack you with the pad. This drill will take away your energy fast. Within 2 minutes you will be breathing hard, not because you are unfit but because your adrenaline has kicked in big time and it feels real. We are now cooking on 6. If you train at this level you are starting to bring the feeling of the street onto the mat.

Level 7 is fighting a no-win situation because the attackers are all over you so fast the aggression turns to frustration, fear and panic. In a real situation you will feel frustration so you have to know how you would handle it and how little of the technical stuff will work under such pressure. This level is best done in groups of 4; one is the target and 3 are attacking armed with mitts and shields. The attackers move around the target verbally attacking the target, then at anytime they attack hitting the target with the shields and focus mitts. Within seconds the target is on the floor unable to fight back as the attackers hold the target down and keep attacking on the ground for say 10-15 seconds.

Level 8 brings all aspects together as in level 7 but this time the target can hit out at the attackers. This drill will kick in your fear of attack but because this time you can hit out the frustration is not so bad. You will still find that you are closed down very quickly and rolling into a ball to protect yourself. You may be fighting one of the attackers on the floor but the other 2 are kicking you all over. We do these drills with full protection and the kicks that are put in on the floor are not hard, but it feels so real that you will be exhausted in seconds.

Level 9. Form a circle. The target stands in the middle eyes closed, full safety gloves, gum shield, etc. All the attackers stand around the target verbally attacking, then one at a time they attack. If the fight goes to the floor it's stopped. The target stands back up and the drill is repeated, by closing their eyes the target is put under greater pressure. Not knowing where the attack is coming from brings the fear to the surface, this is not about winning the fight but handling your fear of the attack.

So is a street fight level 10? No, a lot higher. The shock that hits you is overwhelming because you know it's real. No safety protection, no referee or Instructor to call time. How can you handle your fear telling you that you might just die here on the pavement outside the bus stop? But if you have trained to feel fear and aggression you have a greater chance of dealing with the situation. You can do a lot to understand yourself and how to handle your fears. Anyone who has gone into competition be it Kickboxing, Judo, Thai boxing Sambo or the Total Fight Forum all have to handle the fact that fears build up days, weeks and hours before a fight. To me you're a winner if you can just step in the ring because to handle all your fears and doubts beforehand is a real test.

My good friend Darrin Richardson who has trained and fought in Russia many times still talks about having the feeling of adrenalin weeks before he gets on the plane. Like many good martial artists who keep the pressure on to stay on top have found, the battle with themselves is the hardest one. Once you are on the mat or in the ring, you can let the adrenalin out to help you win.

Everyone one of us has fears and we all handle them in our own way along with aggression. From getting frustrated in a queue at the shops or at traffic lights in the car it's all part of our normal day to day lives. What many of us don't encounter on a daily basis is in your face aggression and because it is something so out of context with our normal day it's hard to handle. I hope you will try out the training drills, I have found that they helped many come to terms with dealing with the fears they have had in a street confrontation. They are not cast in stone. Take them at your own pace, but if you have found them just a little bit uncomfortable just to read, it is time to step into the pool.

Chapter 11

Looking for Spiders

As human beings we may not always make the right decision or judgement about a situation being safe or possibly dangerous. Too many things are waiting to distract us from always making the right choice. But our instincts can override our distraction and switch us onto danger quicker than a traffic warden can write out a parking ticket.

Imagine you are curled up on the sofa at home watching the late night movie, your eyes are fixed to the television screen. It's a great film and to help with the enjoyment you have turned all the lights off to help you concentrate and to get the feeling of being in the cinema. With everything focused on screen you suddenly get a fearful image flash across your view, not on the screen but something in the room. You turn your head to look. It's hard to see in the darkened room, because your eyes have not adjusted from the glare of the television screen yet. You turn the room lights back on and there in the far corner of the room is a spider. Now depending on how you feel about spiders you may pick it up and throw it out the kitchen door or you may wish to introduce it to the heel of your size nines.

I'm sure many of you reading this have experienced something similar to the spider running across the floor. Or an unseen movement that catches the corner of your eye but can make your whole body jump. Your peripheral vision is a very important part of your body's own self defence system, but it is also one of the first things you lose when you are face to face in a confrontation.

It is a sad fact that many victims do not see the attack coming until it is too late. When the fight is all over you, your animal instincts take over. From covering your head with your hands and curling up into a ball or lashing out with everything you've got. Because your peripheral vision is lost in a heated confrontation anything your attacker has decided to throw at you can come unseen. So if we could work at holding onto that highly sensitive peripheral vision longer, it would help us build up our own personal fighting edge.

Some years ago I was taking part in a 3-day martial arts convention in the UK. It had some of the top names from the UK and from around the world teaching. One of the Instructors gave a class on mind and power within the martial arts. Now I have never been one who has had much interest in the so-called deeper meaning of the martial arts. Mainly because many of the people I have met and had to listen to before, remind me of the jazz trombone player who believes he is playing something deep and meaningful, but to me it sounds crap.

Like many things it's the way it's put across. Luckily for me this particular day the Instructor and information were first class. One of the things we covered were some drills on peripheral vision. We were partnered in groups of 4; first 2 people faced me at a distance of about 20 feet and about 10 feet apart. The 2 people facing me were given 10 paper pates each, when the signal was given they had to throw the plate as hard and as fast as they could and I had to block and dodge the incoming plate. I was pleased they were paper plates as many hit the target. The next part of the drill had the fourth person stand in between my 2 plate throwing attackers. This time I was told not to look at the attackers but to look at the person in the middle and not take my eyes off him, but still block and dodge the incoming plates. Some of the plates got through but this time I blocked and dodged many more than the first time about 70% more. This wasn't jazz this was something I could relate to.

The drill with the plates worked because our eyes are more movement sensitive when you respond to the attacks using your peripheral vision. By focusing on the person in the middle and not the two people throwing the plates got us to work on our peripheral vision. Because your eyes are not trying to pick out the detail your peripheral vision picks up the movement, which triggers an automatic dodge or block. In fact the movements we made to avoid the plates became smaller when we used our peripheral vision.

You could look at it this way. If you tried to swat a fly in mid air, your movements will feel slow and awkward as you try so hard to focus on the fast ever changing movements of the fly. But have you ever found yourself reacting to a fly or an insect that is buzzing around your face? Your hand flicks out quickly delivering a backhand that sends the intruder buzzing out of control. We are not very good at judging distance because our eyes are on the front of our face, to get a good break down of distance our eyes would have to be on the side pointing forward. But we are good at feeling distance that is personal space; if we feel threatened we can feel more and more uncomfortable as the distance closes. But we lose a lot if not all of our peripheral vision when face-to-face in a real confrontation. We can really find ourselves fighting in the dark.

To give yourself an idea look at something in front of you. Now roll a piece of A4 paper into a tube, close one eye and look through the tube with the other eye. If this was a violent confrontation what you now see though the end of the tube is all you would see of your attacker. Like a magician that can make a playing card or white dove disappear by getting you to look in the wrong place at the right time. Fear of confrontation can make the whole of the outside world seem to disappear and have you looking in the wrong place, at the wrong time.

So how can we work at not falling into the trap of tunnel vision and losing our visual edge in a real situation? First, if you can relate to what I have been talking about so far then you already have the edge. If you can understand what may happen then you can do something about it. Keep your field of view moving, not just moving your eyes but your head and body to see what is going on around you. Like the plate's, soft focus by looking past and to one side of the attacker then back to the other side. Remember that the rush of adrenalin you will get in a real confrontation will automatically pinpoint what or whom you feel is the threat, but the attack can come from your left or right and behind you as well.

Our eyes are good at picking up left to right movements, but not so good at distance so by changing your view you won't get locked into one person. If you can be tactile at the same time your hands can pick up unseen movements, by using your fence your lead hand will pick up someone moving in front of you as you look to the left to see what his mate is doing.

I know this may sound a little too close for comfort but close is where street fights are won or lost. Your eyes can let you down; your personal perception of the danger you feel you are in is a better guide as to whether or not you are about to be attacked. Like the spider running across the floor switches on a fearful dread, the attacker standing in your face will make you feel the fear but unable to turn on the comfort and safety of your living room lights. You have to take control of the situation quickly. Don't get locked into a staring match, keep scanning around you.

The eye train shuffle

If you ever travel on a train or bus you will understand the eye train shuffle. No one holding eye-to-eye contact, looking at the other passengers but only when they are looking away. It's a way of setting your space and seeing if anyone is a threat. Once you are happy you may switch off and read a book, hopefully this one. But please keep looking around you.

If you feel someone is looking at you and you look straight back at him or her you will get the feeling of tunnel vision. It can become quite intense and one of you will back down because it is a threat, just by breaking long eye contact can take away the threat. Most of this we all understand because we deal with this type of thing daily, but the loss of vision we get when confronted is something we need to control by scanning around us all the time.

I hope you will try out some of the ideas but please only paper plates. To any opticians out there I apologise for the basic description of the working of the human eye and to any up and coming jazz trombone players.

Chapter 12

Men and Women, What Weaker Sex?

It must be said that no matter what your age size or sex everyone has the ability to protect themselves. It is having the will to do something not your size or if you are male or female. Now the ladies reading this might say that's ok for you to say being a man. What do you know? I know what would put a man off and what someone could do to me to stop me in my tracks. But it is true to say what do men understand about the fear many women have walking around the street? And how can a man give them advice on what to do or say to stay safe? That's why I'm keen for women to do more when it comes to passing on their ideas and knowledge to others. As I man I can't see it all from a woman's viewpoint. But I can say this, that some of the most determined people I have trained with and who have shown strength beyond their size have been women.

Any problem I had when I worked on the nightclub door or looking after someone's private party was always with someone smaller than I was. Now it could be alcohol, drugs or their 3 mates standing behind them that gave them the bottle to have a go. Whatever it was they had come to the point that they would not back down. I knew I had a problem not from how big the person was but from how determined they were. I have had the privilege to train with and teach some very determined women who have shown more bottle than many men who have come to train with me. Over the years women have given a lot to the fighting arts taking on all aspects of the arts, from Judo and karate to the hard contact styles of kick boxing, Muay Thai and boxing.

The main thing that comes across that I have found by training with some of these ladies is the spirit that they show in their training is of a high standard. Most of the ladies who have trained with me have at one time been involved in some form of street confrontations. From attempted rape to being beaten up at a bus stop or being punched and kicked by a man after asking him just to move away from a doorway. Maybe women do have a harder time on the streets. They may not be attacked on a daily basis but the threat they generally feel is real. I am ugly enough not to be bothered with the day to day harassment of someone chatting me up in a pub, or have them look at me in an uncomfortable way on the bus going home from work. So are the martial arts covering all the aspects for women when it comes to staying safe on the street? The threat women face from attack may not be the knife wielding monster but the day-to-day fear many face just going about their normal routine.

This type of threat and fear of something that could happen was made very clear to me one day travelling home late one night on the tube. This particular tube station would close all the exits except for the main entrance late at night. So if you wanted to cross to the south side of the station you had to walk over a very dark footbridge. This one night only a hand full of people got off at this stop. Handing in my ticket I thought nothing about walking over the footbridge. As I started walking up the steps I felt very uncomfortable, there was a young lady walking over the bridge - she was about 10 steps in front of me. To walk over the bridge would normally take no longer than 2min but this night it seemed to take hours. I could feel how uncomfortable the lady in front of me felt, about having me walking behind her. I wanted to say to her, *"excuse me. It's OK. I'm not a threat, I'm just on my way home"*. But the fear was so real that to this day I'm convinced that if I had tried to talk to her, just to reassure her, it would have made the situation much worse. So I slowed down to give her time to get across the bridge. By the time I got to the top of the bridge she was on her way down the other side. What made it more intense was that the footbridge had high concrete walls; you could not see to the left or right - it was like a tunnel and your footsteps would echo from one end to the other.

When I got to the other side and started walking down the steps my heart sunk because the lady was taking the same turning I would have to take to get home. The feeling was getting worse. It may seem strange to say but I felt her fear. We seemed to be linked by invisible chains. The faster she walked and the more I slowed down seemed to make no difference to the distance between us. And the feeling of danger she felt from me was getting worse. I could take no more when I got to the bottom of the steps. I did not move for about 10 minutes and when I did I took the other street adding 15 minutes to my walk home. I felt that bad about the situation. As I'm writing this now years later it still makes me feel uncomfortable, just thinking what she must have been feeling and just thinking about how many times this type of situation happens every day.

Every Day

It is hard to understand how we are going to feel about a situation until we find ourselves in one. But most of us can understand the feeling of the fear of danger. I have trained with and talked to some women who want to do something about their fear. When it comes to preparing themselves for the danger they feel on the street the harder and the more real the training the more confident they feel about handling a real situation. Again this is something that comes from inside the individual but it can be developed over time. If the pressure of a situation can happen every day then taking some time to understand yourself and what you can do about it is essential

I am not talking about having great punching and kicking power but more about understanding situations and threat assessment. Most situations can be dealt with by seeing the possible dangers before you have to react in a physical way. What would be the best way to get this information across? Are men the best people to pass on this information or are women better prepared and do they have a better understanding of what women are looking for? For me, I feel it depends on the information given out. Look at it this way, the best female self-defence books on the market is *"Dogs don't know Kung Fu"*, by Jamie O'Keefe. No matter how nice a dress Jamie could get himself into, in no way could he pass himself off as female. It's the information that brings home the true nature of the danger and what you can do about it.

In his book "Unleash the Lioness" Robin Houseman gives a fantastic insight into what women can do, with basic and the hard-hitting truth about fighting back. In just over one hundred pages he makes the truth clearer than many so called women's self defence courses that waffle on about what to do for ages. The danger is having someone teaching self-defence courses in your local sports centre where the idea is a quick profit on a six-week course with poor information. What if the information and content is unworkable? It may make the people on the course feel more confident. But it's dangerous to send them out poorly armed for the real dangers of the street when they may have to face a possibly dangerous situation every day.

Not a Ring Craft?

There are limits and I'm not talking about having women fight in no-holds barred fights against a man stronger and heavier than they are. It would be a mis-match when you're talking about something that is a ring craft. Like all competitions, you set limits for safety reasons. Someone like Sharon Thompson who has taken part in some very hard training sessions (that would have most people making their excuses and walking away) has tested her ability along with the men on the now infamous Animal Day training sessions.

So I was pleased Sharon took some time out to talk to me about the subject and how she feels about training with men.

"Belief in oneself comes from testing yourself and the limits that you are willing to take yourself to. Training with men can build your confidence, like when you find yourself holding your own against them within your training. But fighting someone who is stronger and heavier than you within the confines and rules of a training hall can takeaway your confidence in yourself, so you should always separate the two. In respect to making things work on a street level understanding the threat and how to get away from a situation that could develop out of control very

quickly is more important. I can see how women may feel uneasy about walking into a training hall full of men, but that's taking the first step, I have never really had a problem with that. It makes your training more demanding, making it feel as real as possible can help you control your fear of a situation".

I have been lucky enough to see Sharon demonstrate her striking power and fighting skills many times and I believe that not many people could take a right cross from Sharon and still be able to eat solid food.

How big a monster could you handle?

At this point in time I am very lucky to have some great people to train with, people who are keen to push themselves to the limit. Sevim has been training with me for many years and she is always keen to know if she can get the better of the guys on the mat. Just the fact that she is willing to try demonstrates she has more bottle than a milk float. The guys in the group tower over her, each having more weight in one leg than the whole of Sevim's body. But if she gets her arm around your neck she will put on a choke that will have you fighting for your life. You can punch pull and scratch but she will not let go until you're on the floor tapping for her to stop. In fact it has taken a lot of persuasion to make Sevim understand just how much pain we are in, and if we train for groin and throat attacks Sevim finds it hard to get a partner.

After one particularly hard training session I made the point about just how much courage it takes from the ladies to train with us. If we put it into context just by scaling up the training partners to what someone like Sevim and Liz have to face every time they get on the mat to train with us. It would be like stepping in the ring with the biggest guys from WWF but without the fake kicking and punching. Just think about it. Would you face off someone standing close on 7 feet and weighting 30 stone? I think I would have left with my excuses in the car park along with the smell of burning rubber as I drove off. Weaker sex? I don't think so. By training with the men women can find out just how weak and easily hurt little boys us men can be.

Women taking the lead

So it's great to see people like Liz Clark running ladies self defence course, that are structured to cover women's fear of street violence. With the understanding of having been involved first hand in some very dangerous situations, she can cover what is workable. She is in great demand having been on national television and radio talking about her experiences. She also runs short courses for ladies self defence. It must make the women on the course feel much more comfortable and able to accept the idea that you can do something about your safety, when the information comes from another woman who has had to face her fear. After a short course some of the women may feel they would like to take up the fighting arts, which is great.

But the lead has to come from somewhere. I'm not only talking about the thousands of women who train and enjoy their martial arts every week up and down the country but also the millions of women who have the fear of someone walking behind them. We can't drag people along to take part in some form of self defence training in the same way you can't make people install smoke alarms. The "if only" is always said loudly after the event. And I don't think the answer is getting people to do a six weeks' Karate or any other martial arts course. They have to be structured for what people are going to find happening on the streets today. Men can play a part but I feel women have the greater opportunity to do something for women's self defence in a big way.

I am talking about how people train women and deal with the problems of size but the same does go for the guys. And I do not want to labour the point too much more, but after training with many small men and women and also some guys that could stand in as King Kong stuntman. It is true to say that it's the size of fight in the person not the size of the person. Women like Sevim, Liz and Sharon Thompson are people who many women can relate to about the fears they may have walking down the street.

I have always felt that if something can work for someone who may feel at a disadvantage in their size then that's what I would like to work with. In his book *"I thought you'd be Bigger"*, Kevin O'Hagan demonstrates the point that you can bring down the bigger man. Kevin is smaller than most people would think of just going by his reputation as a fighter. But this has given him strength and focus when it comes to the point of making it work for the smaller person. Myself being someone who not so much tips the scales on the high side more like pushes them through the floor when I stand on them. I stand over 6 foot and one thing that I can add to that size question is the fact it means nothing to who will win.

Chapter 13

YOU MUST BE CHOKING

Apart form poking someone in the eyes or crushing their testicles a good way to stop an attack is to stop them from breathing. How long for, well that's up to you? But your airway is a sensitive organ. Any happy cyclist with fly's all over his face will tell you that he will slam on the brakes and be coughing like a 40 a day smoker if just one little fly flew into his mouth and went down his throat.

So how much damage and discomfort do you feel a person would have if you pushed your thumb hard into their Adam's apple, or grabbed their windpipe and squeezed it as if you were holding a safety rope? The person would crumble with no more effort than it takes to throw a ball. Before I go on I must make the point that chokeholds are not that easy to put on someone who is still firing on all cylinders. It takes time and a lot of skill to work a good choke-hold well, but striking, poking with your fingers or punching to the throat can be learnt and done very quickly. Most people who talk about using chokes as a controlling technique have to work to a high safety level because if a good choke is on you can move from control to death very quickly.

Before we take a look at some of the training ideas you can work through to get you thinking about striking the throat. You may be thinking what can I do to stop a person who is choking me. You will find the best way to get out of a choke-hold is not to let it get put on in the first place. Now you may be saying. *"Who is this smart ass? That's obvious"* Then why do people believe and teach that you can get out of a choke? When a good choke is on, one thing you can be sure of is you no longer have to worry about the next payment on the mortgage. If you are thinking, "I could grab the attacker's groin, punch, kick or pull his little finger back until he lets go". Please, stop reading for a moment, go out side check that the sky is blue and the trees are green, yes we are home from our intergalactic trip and are back on the plant earth.

Ok just think about this for a minute. You only have seconds left if someone is choking you. Add the panic you will feel and the last breath you had is disappearing fast. Your hands will instinctively work on the attacker hands to try and break the hold, or your hands will shoot out trying to hit the attacker in the face. Being in a position of control the attacker will move his head away from your attack getting stronger as he feels you getting weaker, and your time to do anything effective is running out. As someone who is interested in practical self defence training, teaching what will or will not work in a real situation for me is the key. It is very important to draw the line between the art of thinking what you can do and the reality of what you are able to do. If you are shown a technique for getting out of a grab, choke or hold then you work with a partner to practise the technique. As you work you are learning the key points of the technique and versions of the technique. To make it harder you can operate degrees of resistance, working the drill in this way, helps you find out what works under pressure.

It is amazing how many techniques fall at the first sign of resistance. When your partner's leg, arm, head or wrist does not move the way you had expected it to, a form of panic sets in. Simple ideas such as pushing your chin into your chest to stop the attacker from getting a good hold around your throat. Or covering your head with your hands looking like a high boxing guard will also stop for a time the choke or strangle being put on well. This will give you a little more fight time. Dropping your weight as long as you have covered your neck will also make the job of the attacker much harder once the attack is on. But all this must be done before the choke or strangle is on, because without the cover YOU ONLY HAVE SECONDS.

Who says that you have to be big to fight back?

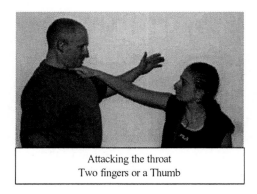

Attacking the throat
Two fingers or a Thumb

Choke or Strangle

Basically a choke will cut off the supply of air getting into your lungs so at best if you can deal with the discomfort you have about 30 seconds to 1 minute of fight time left. If you are being strangled the blood supply to your brain is being cut off and you can be unconscious in 8 to 10 seconds. With a striking blow to the throat you can be incapacitated for minutes with violent coughing and will be unable to deal with anything else apart from getting your air supply back. A strike to the side of the neck will interfere with the blood supply to the brain and you will be unconscious before you hit the ground. I have experienced all of the above in training at sometime or another and luckily for me it has been with people who are training partners and will stop. When the chokes, strangles or strikes have made their target I have found it impossible to fight back. This is a serious business and in no way should you under estimate the danger you give or receive from these techniques.

Working on that second?

I would love to give you a technique that would help you pull out from a choke or strangle once on but I can't. You can only work with the gap between the hold being locked on and the seconds before, looking to do something in that first second of reflex action you have. In the same way if you stick yourself with a pin your natural reflex is to pull away from the pain. So seeing someone reaching to grab you round the neck should have you pushing his or her hands away as quickly as you can. If you are grabbed from the front or from behind and you are not being held around the throat, then you will be able to use that kick, punch, strike, bite or head-butt to get your attacker off you.

Like the boxer who would have loved to have seen and dodged the punch that knocked him out, or the no holds barred fighter who wished he had closed the gap and not let his opponent get that choke on. People like the trained boxer or no rules competition fighter, train very hard for any fight they may enter and know the price of making a mistake in the ring. Just one second's misjudgement will have the referee stopping the fight, all the hard hours, days and weeks building up to the fight gone in a second.

In the street, you may have no time to build up to a fight; your fighting rounds are the awareness and threat assessment I have been talking about. Any mistakes you make now could end with a punch in the mouth, a screwdriver in the chest or someone grabbing you around the throat, and as you lapse into unconsciousness you are silently dragged away.

So the following training drills are to be done with care but also with some degree of discomfort for you to get the reflex action working, and feel just how little time you have. For safety you must always use the tap rule, which is as soon as you feel uncomfortable you tap your partner or the floor to stop the drill, your partner must release the hold the instant you tap.

Feeling is believing you can only deal with something when you appreciate how big the problem can be.

One-handed attacks.

Stand in front of your partner and place two fingers at the base of their throat, keeping your arm straight have your partner walk into you. Your partner will feel uncomfortable with this; to some people just having someone touching their throat will be enough to have them backing away. Do the same again but this time just give a gentle push with your finger as they move in, your partner will move back quickly coughing on reflex. So just think about being grabbed by someone and thrusting your two fingers hard at your attacker throat.

Stand in front of your partner with one hand covering their throat now close your fingers. Gentle squeeze the windpipe, remember stop as soon as your partner taps this is very uncomfortable. Just think that if you did this to an attacker and squeezed as hard as you could, do you think they would have a respiratory problem or what? You could use any combination to attack the windpipe grabbing, pushing with your fingers, fist, and side of your hand, thumb or even a ballpoint pen. Again these ideas are dangerous and you should be very careful in your training, but if you need to use them to protect yourself you use them as hard as you can.

Getting out of a one-handed attacks

If you get struck in the throat or the side of the neck, the truth will be that you will fall to the floor. If you are still on your feet you will be unable to do much about protecting yourself. Your instincts on the floor could be to roll into a ball, if standing you may crouch down covering your head, you need time to recover. How much time do you have? Well your attacker is the only person who will decide that. Most people will tuck their chin down when grabbed around the throat. This does hold off the pressure if someone is grabbing your throat and your instinct will have you grabbing the attacker's arm. If you can make your grab into a fast pull on your attacker's arm this again will help you get that important gap. When seconds count you need to attack the eyes, nose, your attacker's throat. You have to have more aggressive than a pit bull.

Smothered/ grabbed front or behind

To see how shocking this type of attack can be; stand behind your partner, bring your hand around and cover their nose and mouth. Close down hard pressing your thumb and first finger around their nose, your partner will find it very hard to breathe through their mouth. In their panic to breathe they will find the suction made with them breathing in will hold your hand tighter onto their face. You can do the same thing standing in front and attacking by pushing them back against a wall or doorway.

To feel the panic, have your partner close their eyes. Don't tell them when you are going to attack. When you do pull them in, hold them close to your body and release when they tap.

How do you get them off, or more to the point how do you get your next breath? If you can get your teeth onto the attacker's hand bite as hard as you can, and I mean down to the bone. If you can get one or both of your hands on to the attacking arm pull as hard as you can to make a gap and drop your weight taking your feet off the floor if you have to. If you are on your feet you are giving him leverage to put on the pressure or walk you backward. Don't help him, make it feel like he is dragging a heavy sack of coal, but a sack that is kicking, biting and scratching for his eyes, face and balls.

Look you cannot work these ideas as if you are following a set of instructions to put together a coffee table. In an easy going environment you can make anything work even the most complicated movements can be performed. But with the panic of a real attack and the threat of death you will be as flexible as a plank of wood. You must use this safety time for training with someone who can put you under pressure and you trust to find out what it feels like and what will work. And you should understand that you are in deep shit if you give your attacker one or two seconds before you have done anything about it.

Jokes, Strangles and Chokes

One of the biggest jokes I have seen within my training in the fighting arts (and there have been many) was seeing an Instructor showing a student how to get out of a rear choke and stranglehold. His arm was right around the students' throat pushing into the windpipe and his forearm pressing into the side of the students' neck cutting off the blood supply. The Instructor had also linked his arm and with his left hand was pushing the students' head forward. To get out of the hold he told the student to reach up and grab the Instructors little finger and pull it back, then moving back under the arm which was then locked the student could kick the Instructor in the ribs. The crowd thought it was amazing, fantastic skill and real technique. No one coughing or gagging. No one dropped down in pain no one fell to the floor. What bollocks. *"This is a dangerous technique"* he said. No its dangerous because he was putting it forward as workable. If he were selling out of date sandwiches to the public he would be arrested for endangering people's health.
You can work on chokes and strangles with a partner and if you wish to try out any technique you can do it safely without the pressure of a full chokehold. But you must understand the limits,

and when I said the only sure way of getting out of a choke or strangle is not to let it get put on in the first place, you will find is true. People's instinct to protect automatically soft parts of their body will keep most of the first movements of an attack towards those parts away. But only if the threat is seen. Like the footballer will stand in a line protecting the goal from a free kick but will cover his groin just in case. The same football will bring him down if it hit him unseen.

Most people have the image of the two handed front attack, with

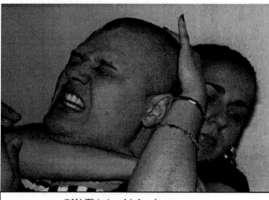

OK! This is a bit harder to get on, but impossible to get out of

the victim being grabbed around the throat. If the attacker is strong and determined then most things talked about when it comes to breaking free by taking away the attacker's hands are wrong. As you have felt in some of the drills the slightest pressure will induce such fear and panic you are left in weak desperation. Like a drowning man will be clutching at straws or push the lifeguard underwater to reach for that next breath, his desperation is working against him and he will die.

The time you have to get free is beforehand, as it is with anything to do with self-protection. Do not let anyone tell you that you can get out of a full on choke/strangle hold. If anything good can be said, it's if someone grabs you, you are in no doubt about having to fight back.

Chapter 14

A-Round of Golf, Anyone?

Punches, strikes and Problems

Without doubt the most physical contact made within a fight is with your hands, from pushing away your attacker to slapping, scratching and punching. Also finger wagging and pointing with a hard stare, which can show the intention of someone who is about to attack. The hands can inflict damage with both open hand strikes or with closed fists. They can grab, hold and push. If you also add all the more colourful finger and hand gestures so often used as precursors to an attack the combinations seem endless. So how can we practise striking within the confines of a real street fight when time and the space available are short? And how can we understand and work around the pre-fight hand contact made by many attackers as they threaten or pacify us before unleashing their attack?

We are lucky to have many pieces of equipment available for us to practice our strikes and punches on. With this equipment we can strike as hard as

Focus mitts – great fun and endless training ideas

we like without damaging our training partners and upsetting any egos or friendships. Equipment has moved on a lot over the years from the basic punch bag to pre-shaped bags and pads, angle bags for upper cuts, curved hook and jab pads and body shields.

From the simple ceiling hook to support your bag we how have folding, deluxe and chain swivel brackets. Now with water filled bases we can get the pre-shaped head and torso of a man to practise hard punches to the jaw or nose or striking or grabbing the head or throat. I think it's great fun and great to see anything that will get people trying out their striking skills. Who knows where it will end? Just think in the future you may be able to buy your own interactive fight time android, just program in the fighting style and the degree of difficulty and you're off.

Hitting Hard. Like most things in life anything we want to do well takes practice. Some people seem to have a natural ability when it comes to punching but anyone can learn to hit hard. It's a matter of breaking down the key points that can get you hitting hard.

A boxer with a knockout punch is said to punch his own body weight. Punch your weight and make it fast and you will get a powerful punch. You generate more power when you drive your weight across the target before your punch or strike makes contact. When you make contact keep driving through, making a punch or strike a fast push.

Punch bag for power

A-Round of Golf Anyone?

We could look at sports outside the fighting arts to help us improve the discipline we practice. Gymnasts for their flexibility and grace, a Footballer for co-ordination, control and powerful kicking. The Rugby player for teamwork, power and stamina (also a good pint and a good singsong), Racing, the jockey for um? Not sure at the moment, but the horses are nice and the jockeys do wear nice colours.

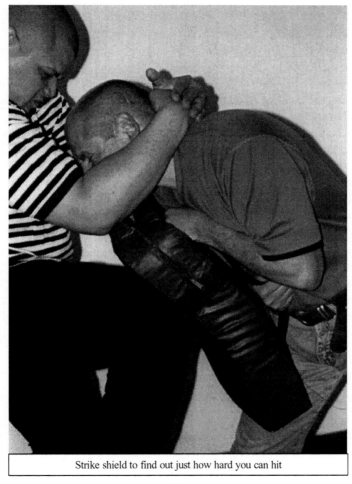

Strike shield to find out just how hard you can hit

One of the best training examples I know for improving power on strikes or punches is to take a look at a Golfer playing off the tee. He or she generates amazing power driving a ball hundreds of yards, with a technique of driving through the ball. Not stopping the club at the tee, staying relaxed they drive their hips and body past the ball. All this giving a maximum arc and acceleration to the club to drive the ball. (I do apologise to any golfers out there for my description of a golf swing). I am not an avid golfer myself, in fact the first time I can remember playing golf was on a family holiday when I was about eight. Bringing back the club to hit the ball as hard as I could the only thing I hit was my brother who was standing behind me. The club hit him full in the face, and I ran off crying at the sight of his face covered in blood. (That might have started my interest in martial arts)

Staying relaxed is the hardest part of power punching. Most people will tense up. The more tension you have the slower you will move. With all the equipment I mentioned before you can practice building up a powerful arsenal and the only way to find out if you can hit hard is to hit something. If you can get the first punch off in a street fight you are fighting at your best, or lets say your first punch is likely to be the strongest because you had some time to set it up. But your best shot can be lost if the person in front of you has grabbed you or just poked his finger in your chest. You no longer have a clean shot. Hands, arms, elbows, jackets, tables and chairs all seem to get in the way. How can we work on powerful striking and punching ideas in the close and personal areas of a street fight?

Building your own Android

After getting your basic hard punch working on the bag, the next step is to build up your ability to hit back when a good punching or striking range has been lost. If you miss the first time it is more than likely your strikes will have to work their way through a sea of uncontrolled attacks. Your strikes and punches now have to work when the distance available may be just a few inches. To give yourself some idea of what this may feel like put on a coat or jacket do it up and stand in front of your punch bag. Pull your right arm out of the sleeve so it trapped inside, with your left-hand hold the punch bag, now try punching with your right hand as hard as you can. You will find it frustrating because of the lack of movement you have and how weak your strikes feel and that's good. Not only will you understand how important it is to get your best strike off first but also how little you have to work with when it goes wrong.

Your strikes become strong pushes and grabs, if the fight is this close then you are going to also think about biting and using you hands and fingers to poke and grip. Attacking eyes, throat, ears and groin. Outside the ring there is no such thing, as a clean fight.

Until someone invents the training android the next best thing is to put your self under pressure. By adding tricks like the jacket or restricting the movement you have around the punch bag you can do a lot for your personal training. But the next step is to not only feel the restriction of close striking but also to now add the danger that if you make a mistake you are a target. I am lucky to have my own personal androids that go by the futuristic name of Tim and Tony. They have both trained with me for a number of years and always seem keen when it comes to using me for target practice. Like any form of contact training it takes a little time to build up your confidence but it is something you have control over. No one should push you into something you do not feel happy with. But if you take it step by step you will amaze yourself in just how short a time you can turn up the pressure.

Taking the first step

Keep it safe. Wearing the right protective equipment will help you with taking that first step along with slowly introducing faster and harder strikes. Try out these two basic training ideas. Both are done with both partners fighting on their knees. This restricts the fighters from backing off and if the fighters fall over they have the safety of being close to the floor.

You should always have fun with your training. That's the great thing about training in a group or at a club with the safety of knowing its ok to make a mistake here with people who are looking to find out the same things about themselves as you are. I often tell my students that this is play but from play you can feel the reality and the harder the play the more you can cope with the reality.

1st Drill One person is attacking, the other is controlling. The attacker can punch for the head or body. Because you are on your knees you will find it hard to get any power in your punch at first. But as you are just starting off that's a good thing. The person controlling grabs the attacker keeping their head tucked in and close to the attacker. You will find that as the punches and strikes have to work their way through very small gaps to the target, the strikes become hard pushes. Trying to keep upright is also difficult, it does become a bit of a tug of war and very quickly fatigue sets in so start with just one-minute rounds.

2nd Drill Both partners attacking. You will find that the first few seconds are when the hardest punches land on their target. If you are the one who is on the receiving end you will soon get to grips with the fact that to move in and close down the attacks is your best option. Then working in your strikes from a closing down position, because if you keep dodging side to side out of the way of the attacks, the attacks just keep coming. Again take it easy start with one-minute rounds and build up the pressure a bit at a time.

The good thing about the above drills is that you find out in a safe way just how little time you have when it comes to getting the first strike in. Also you start to feel the panic of an attack and the body's automatic kick of adrenaline that will make you feel you don't want to turn up the pressure anymore. It is a personal thing and no one should tell you to do more, but the first step to finding out what works under pressure is the hardest. If you can get over your first concerns of contact training you will find yourself willing to take on more.

Adding Problems

You can make the drills your own just by adding more ideas to make it that little bit harder each time. When you have tried the drills a few times start them off different ways, say one partner tries pushing and shoving as the other attacks. Have no start time. It begins when someone throws the first punch. Or start the drill with your eyes closed. You could allow head-butting or biting. Its your choice, all of which you can do in a controlled manner. But the big one is with controlled aggression. You may be in a club but if you feel aggression from your partner the timed minute of the drill seems to disappear and you think to yourself are we training or is this real?

I always tell my students that attack is better than defence. It is the basic truth when it comes to looking at street violence. But if you are willing to test yourself in your training by adding pressure the greater your confidence to walk away from a confrontation in the street. Because you know how far you are willing to go and how far you push yourself in your training. It makes the person jumping up and shouting at you over a parking space just not worth the effort. Remember take the training drills slow and work with a partner if you can but you can cover a lot of ground with just a punch bag and a few ideas.

Kicking for the pavement

I have to give you all a bit of bad news; life is not fair. Not everything we want to do is possible. Not everything we dream of can come true; you may be a better cook than Delia Smith or the best new thing in TV quiz show hosts but who gets the job? Richard Whitely. Like I said sometimes life is not fair. For me, to dream of getting high enough off the ground to perform a jump spinning kick and hit a target higher than four feet off the ground is as likely as a damp firework giving pleasure on bonfire night. That's ok with me. After all my years of training I can come to terms with the fact that for me kicking above the waist is no longer a goal.

This takes away nothing for my admiration for people who can do fantastic gymnastics and have amazing kicking skills. After all, everyone should admire the talent and skill of others. It opens our minds to what an individual can achieve, from writing a great piece of music to an actor giving a great performance in a Theatre. So please don't think I am knocking all the hard work a person puts into getting their jump kick higher or kicking on one leg for 5 minutes. In the right environment it's exciting and great fun but on the pavement or inside a night-club it's dangerous.

I do believe that when dealing with a situation which could explode in a second into a violent attack your response must be reliable. With all the pressure building up around you how confident would you feel about making that jump? This is not to say all kicking is not worth using or capable of dealing with an attacker on the street. It's finding what kick has the greatest chance of working. How many kicks do you feel you could perform if your attacker was standing 6 inches in front of you? Or a 6 foot 16 stone very angry man was running at you across the dance floor, just because he's been looking for a fight all night and fuelled with a belly full of alcohol has decided it's you?

The Tap, Tap of disappointment

If you are committed to stopping an attack with your feet then the kicks have to be one off and powerful. You have to separate the tap, tap kicking of the demonstration (with only the resistance of air to stop you making the target.) from the hard and powerful whack of stopping someone in their tracks or the kicking power to drive their legs from under them. You can train both but which one would you use? For me the kick that comes up with the goods is the Thai kick, which is quick and very powerful and for closer attacks knees, shin kicks and foot stamps. I am not a Thai boxer, and a Thai Instructor may throw up his hands in horror at my description and less than technical breakdown of the kick so I apologise now. But I have found the link with the Thai kick driving the weight right through the target delivers great power. Also if someone has never kicked before it's a kick they can pick up the basic idea of very quickly. Again I always prefer kicking at a low level. Not that a student in time is not capable of developing the skill to kick high. More to the point it comes down to finding the space, time and opportunity in a real confrontation.

One person who has influenced me a lot about kicking over the years is Peter Consterdine of the British Combat Association. Like his striking and power punch ideas, they are simple but when he makes contact the results are devastating. It was one of the first BCA courses that I went to when I witnessed Peter demonstrate his low swinging kick. No fancy name, he just described using his leg like a heavy log. He talked about the practicalities of high kicks and the fingertip rule. The fingertip rule being if someone is standing with their arms by their sides the area you should aim your kicks at just below their fingertips. With that he demonstrated the point. No tap, tap with Peter, just a powerful charge and whack he took the unsuspecting person's legs away. With no time to break the fall he hit the ground like a sack full of potatoes. From that day on I changed my outlook completely towards kicking on the street. I found that by kicking out the old ideas I had believed in and had been taught over the years as workable, so much more just fell into place, please excuse the pun.

Just pick one

If you could bear with me for a bit on this idea just for this chapter if you like, there are only two kicks in the world. Are you still reading? The kick you want to use against an attacker and the one he MAY use to attack you. What you have to do is find one from the many that you can rely on and train the kick to hit hard. Remember a kick on the street is more than likely to be in your face as you are on all fours getting up after being punched in the face.

I find it interesting when people talk about using the leg for greater reach and power, when reach is not the problem in a fight because your attacker will be close enough to shave you if he had the time. As for power, having held a pad for many intricate kicks, not only does the power not live up to the exciting look of the kick, I still have students who can palm strike harder.

No, if you're going to kick it has to be hard. Again a Thai boxer hits with massive power and conditions their legs to take unbelievable punishment. If you held a pad for a Thai boxer not only will he rock your whole body with the power, he will hit hard every time and from a cold start. No lining up. No getting ready, just whack. It is unlikely that our training partners will let us kick them in the face with full power so hitting a pad with full power is as close as most will get to testing their kick. So test yourself. Have someone hold a pad for you now you have to kick the pad 10 times and so hard your partner feels like giving the pad to someone else after 5 hits. Find out from all the kicks you know which one will hit 10 out of 10 times hard, without lining up the kick and from a cold start.

Then just think what your score would be if you had to do it under the pressure of a real attack. Then add the fingertip rule. Most people will bring their arms up and flinch back. Now your target is moving and his arms are in the way. Are you thinking about how many times you missed the pad and may be life is unfair sometimes? Sometimes taking away make's you stronger. It's better to find out in training than on the street. I have been training in the fighting arts for over 20 years. If I look back over the time and the reasons I first went on the mat; 10 years I wasted on the fancy, the fantastic, wanting the TV and film images to work for me on the 290 bus home from Hammersmith.

Then it was, *"you need to stretch Alan, get the kick higher, lock it out on the target, you have to counter that attack with this technique, more combinations, more counters."* They made it seems that you are going to be attacked hundreds of different ways on the street and you need a different response for every one.

Have you heard this one before? A technique for every possible attack is all well and good if your attacker is in no hurry. It's the Golden egg, the topping off a meal with too much garnish trying to make the unpalatable taste nice to make it work on the street. Take away the garnish, just work with the salt and pepper.

Kick from the fence

Ok I'm sorry if I've been sounding off a bit at all the kickers out there and maybe some are getting a bit pissed off with my view. Like I said at the beginning I do admire what some people can do and the enjoyment they give to others and get themselves from demonstrating their skill. But whatever system you practice they all have to fall into two parts: the art or the practical. You can enjoy all of the system you train in and take it as far as you want to, as long as you are prepared to look and see that other systems may have some ideas more workable on a street level.

The time you have to perform a kick on the street is very small. If you work from the fence idea of attack you find the room you have to manoeuvre is about the size of a telephone box. So to commit to a kick outside the reach of your lead hand, say 3 feet, you will have to kick at the target when they are moving in or you will have to slide or step towards them. I am not saying it's impossible but the speed and distance you have to judge will be unfamiliar and will call for a high degree of skill. For me kicking range is when I can touch the person with my lead hand because I am then 100% sure I will make contact. From a swinging kick (based on the Thai kick) off my rear leg to damage or take their legs from under them. Off the front leg I will use the edge or heel of my foot to attack the knee or shin I don't care whatever hits first. If the person is side on and so close my lead leg is behind theirs I will bring my lead arm up

If your attacker kicks you in the street, it's when you are down

under their chin and take them back over my lead leg. This might not be a kick, more like a trip. I'm not sure what you call it but I'm controlling their leg and taking them down.

A good pair of shoes or boots will add a lot of damage to your target, a good strong kick to the shins can drop your attacker to the floor. Using the edge or heel of your shoes to scrape down the shin or stamp onto the foot can tear skin and break bone. Try out some of the ideas. If you feel that you need to improve your kicking power try out your local Thai boxing club. We have some top people here in the UK. You should always look around for the right product and use that information to improve yourself. Thai boxing will not answer all your needs for street fighting but it will show you explosive kicking power.

And done again

Again

Chapter 15

Armed to the teeth, but with no time to bite.

If it were legal to carry firearms, would you feel safe? If you could walk to the shops with a samurai sword strapped to your back, would you feel that no one would even think about attacking you? If you trained in the martial arts for 10 years, would you feel safe? You may feel safe, but, would you have time to use the above?

Let's say you are armed to the teeth, and walking along minding your own business. When from nowhere, you are attacked, (by 3 members of the local boots, alcohol and drug association). What would you do? Would you shoot one of your attackers with the Magnum, cut the second to pieces with your sword, then treat the third to a lesson in ground fighting? Brushing yourself down, you look at your attackers, now recovering on the pavement, and tell them. *"They messed with the wrong man this time".*

More to the point, confident that no one is about to attack you with all that back up you are carrying you turn a corner, and from nowhere, a Neanderthal grabs you by the throat, pushes you against a wall and demands all your worldly possessions. The Magnum is still asleep in your pocket; the last thing the sword cut was your finger when you played with it in your bedroom. You could beat him to a pulp on the ground, if only he would let go of your throat. And give you five minutes to get your breath back. To him, you feel as dangerous as a newborn baby, who is desperately looking around, for something to suck.

It's no good having the firepower of a small private army, or the fighting ability that 10 years of hard training can achieve, if you think that you would have time to react after, if you let your attacker thrown the first punch. You could be in line to learn a painful lesson. Let me put it this way. If you were told that someone was coming to get you, and would kill you on sight, then you would have time to start making plans. (How much is a one-way ticket to Acapulco?) If you locked your front door, would this give you enough time to call the police, before your would-be attacker breaks the door down and is now about to kill you? You may have enough time to set up an ambush. Time to check your gun, and clean and oil all the moving parts, putting a coffee table against the door would give you more time. With your chair as far away from the door as possible, using a table lamp to light the target area, you sit back and wait.

You can hear him coming, so you take aim. As he breaks down the door you open fire. Everything moves in slow motion. You hit him with so much lead, you find yourself thinking. *"If this guy ever survives this, he could work part time as a pencil"*. So the time to prepare for an attack is before it happens.

I'm not talking about a ring fight or an arranged meeting between two people to sort out a long-standing problem. Today we are bombarded with weapons or self-defence alarms that we are told will help us if we find ourselves in trouble. In fact many people carry things around with them that they will tell you they would use if faced with an attack.

With all this would you be safe?

The problem with carrying anything you feel you have to depend on can become a self-inflicted nightmare. Think about how you would feel if you go to use it only to realise you have left it at home on the kitchen table or in the boot of your car. Don't get me wrong I would use anything that came to hand at the time from an ashtray in a bar to a milk bottle left in the street. But I no longer carry around with me anything you would think of as a weapon, because unless it's in your hand all the time you won't have time to use it.

Lets say you are a trained knife fighter. I'm not talking about the swinging around with a knife in one hand and a fan in the other crap. I'm thinking of the person who trains for street fights and a person who would not give a shit about punching more holes in you with a knife, than you would throw punches or kicks at a punch bag. This type of fighter would have the weapon ready any time they wanted to attack; anyone willing to do this is willing to kill you.

You will mainly only be able to use what you have with you all the time: your hands, feet, elbow, knees and teeth. Anything else can be lost, left behind or taken away from you. Because you get the feeling of strength by having this object with you, without that support you can crumble.

The best way I can put this idea forward is to think of an aggressive driver, his weapon being the car. He is surrounded by a metal box, which can move faster than a cheetah running for its next meal. With windows to see danger and locks on the doors to keep danger out and a powerful engine to out run any problems. If he cuts you up in traffic and you sound your horn in disapproval he and the car will turn into a monster. The roar of the engine and the scream of the tyres are the monster's battle cry, With headlights flashing like the hard stare of a wild animal he and his car have become the beast. By driving close he is attacking your space like a boxer throwing a jab, as you move to the side he pushes past like a rugby forward breaking through the line. As he waves his two-fingered salute from his window and races off in the distance his number-plate reads HARD 666?

You may be very angry with the monster driver but because you are driving the type of car that the speed from 0 to 60 can be measured by an egg timer, you cannot catch him. Oh dear, now you are angry and frustrated. Why have you got a crap car? Ok its good to carry the kids and you can easy load it up with a month's shopping, but for catching monsters it's crap. Now look your luck's in, you can see the monster pulling into a petrol station. With your anger meter in the red you pull into the petrol station like Saint George about to attack the dragon. Pulling the monster from his car your verbal attack is unleashed calling him all the names under the sun and threatening him that if you see him again you will smash him and his car to pieces.

We may feel safe in the car

But once the door is open you are trapped

When you stop shouting you find the monster has turned into a mouse a weak and squeaking mouse. You no longer feel like Saint George that's righting the wrongs you feel more like a bully who picks on the weak. As you lower the mouse back into his car and onto his driving seat you watch him drive off and his number-plate reads SAD 222.

So what has this got to do with not carrying a knife, rape alarm or a sock full of coins? Well the monster in the car when attacked outside the safety of his metal box and no longer having the bodywork and speed for protection feels the fear of being out his safety zone. If you rely on having something with you to protect yourself: one you may not have it with you at the time so your fear of the situation is worsened. Two and more to the point, in a real situation you may find you have no time to use it. Your reliance on a weapon can bring down your level of awareness.

Training with weapons has its place and an understanding of how some people will use a weapon is helpful. But if your faith is placed in something that is strapped to your side or carried in a pocket or hand bag, could you get your hands on it in time? Will you have it with you all the time? How would you cope without it? People can scream blue murder if they run out of milk and have to drink black coffee for one morning. How would they cope with a rapist and find their pepper spray had been left at home?

When I used to carry that little something extra (you know just in case) it was sometime before I realised that I was more fearful of not having the item with me than being attacked. I could be half way down the street to meet up with friends and feeling ok, when I would realise my little something extra was not with me and I would panic. I had to go all the way home to get it, or have the feeling of being vulnerable all evening without it. My fear of being attacked was strong, and it was made worse by putting my faith in something. Not only was I fearful of attack but now I was fearful about not being ready.

You can only fight back with what you have with you at the time, and your best weapon is being aware of any person or situation you find yourself with or in at any time. Feeling in danger is the time to do or use something, do something as simple as walking away from the situation. If the threat you feel is getting greater then use anything that comes to hand. One night my wife and I heard a noise down stairs, I got out of bed and grabbed something off the bedside table. I turned on the light and ran down the stairs determined that who ever was down there was going to get what I had in my hand rammed into their throat.

Mind you the sight of a fat very pale white fleshed screaming man wearing just a pair of pants looming out of the dark at them may have been enough anyway? After sometime spent checking the house all the rooms, cupboards and even the fridge (God knows who I was going to find in the fridge) it turned out to be a false alarm. When I looked down and opened my hand to see what killing machine I had pick up from the bedside table to destroy the enemy with, I found I had a plastic hairbrush.

Awareness at all times, gives you time and is the best weapon you can have.

Chapter 16

Cross Training finding out what works

No one system has all the answers. Put boxing with judo, Thai boxing with grappling. Mix any together and that will give you an idea of the weakness in each.

Determination or Technique

The main point being would you be prepared to do anything to beat your attacker? What would you consider too much to stop someone from attacking you? It is wrong to give yourself limits, if you do end up fighting back because someone has decided to make you their next victim. Life on the streets today is cheap. People can and do kill for very little. Man glassed in the face; Woman raped on her way to work; man beaten for his pension, any could be a headline of any newspaper. As I said before most situations can and should be avoided by using awareness techniques. But the key to fighting back must be your determination to do so. If you are determined you can get though that one thing that will stop your attacker.

It is not a matter of taking a physical fight up in steps. It's a matter of fighting with everything you have in one go. If I told you by pushing your finger into your attacker's eye so hard you could feel the back of the eye socket and taking sight from that eye forever, would you do it? Could you do it? And when would you do it? I know the above can turn the stomach. But the point has to made that the physical act of pushing a finger hard into someone's eye is not hard. The hard part is having the determination to do it. It's not having lots of fighting techniques, just one thing with determination can get great results. When I was a boy living at home with my parents we had a Jack Russell dog; Buster was small but had one weapon like all dogs: teeth. One game Buster liked to play was fighting with an old leather strap. Once he got his teeth in it, the idea of letting go was not in his rulebook.

You could pick him up by the strap, with his teeth locked in place he would still pull with his neck muscles sending his body into uncontrolled movements. The only way to stop him was to lower the strap so his paws were back on the ground and letting go of the strap. And saying *"OK boy you win"*. He would then jump on your lap and lick your face until you played the game again.

We all have this ability to fight and at a level we may think as nightmarish. It's finding the level at which we are willing to take that step. If we can understand the way danger may come at us we can move aside and let it pass. If we can understand and believe in ourselves we can deal with any problem.

Understanding yourself and the level at which you are capable of switching on your aggression comes by finding your own leather strap. Teaching yourself to fight is easy, you can get it from a book, just like learning to swim but at what point will you put the book down and get wet? If you work in an area where you are face to face with confrontation on a daily basis I'm sure you find some form of workout helps you put your level of ability into perspective. It is not easy to think about switching yourself on to the fact that you may have to fight back along with thinking, *"should I hit now? Am I strong enough? And what if it goes wrong?"*

For me one of the most rewarding parts of training in the fighting arts is meeting people who are willing to exchange ideas and who openly promote the idea that you can learn from everyone. So why do some people feel it's such a taboo to think of taking on other people's ideas? If something is better why not change? Outside the world of martial arts we are happy to get help or better information. I, like many people, drive a car, but please don't expect me to understand how the engine works. I am writing this book on a computer, but what goes on inside this cream coloured box, from keyboard to screen is a mystery.
So when the car breaks down, or the computer screen goes blank, I am happy to get outside help. Mike repairs my car and Tony laughs at my pathetic attempts to understand the computer.

Every time I train with or teach someone, I learn, and if I'm shown something better I will change. If someone can show me a better way, then I would be mad not to listen. No one person can have all the answers, but everyone you meet can take you that bit nearer. From the outset this is what I wanted to do with the Self Protection Association, because inside I felt that there was a lot missing from my training. The problem I had in the past was that I knew that 90 percent of my training would not work in the street. So for years I had doubt and the most uncomfortable part at the time, was teaching people with this doubt inside me.

Cross training has taken off big time when it comes to what people are looking for. Whatever answer anyone may give now, I am sure they went to their first martial arts class because they felt unsafe, and having a black belt would make them feel more confident. Unfortunately it only gives them confidence within the group they are training with at the time. Step outside that group and the training and fighting ideas fall apart quicker than a newspaper in the rain.

Stepping outside

Over the years I have found that stepping outside of what feels comfortable within my own training has brought me the greatest sense of achievement. It doesn't matter if you cannot do the basic drills within a new or strange training environment. Or if the most junior member of the club is beating the pants off you. The fact that you are there, trying, is the most important thing. Putting yourself on the line is both the test and the achievement. Some of the Instructors and their students I have trained with have made me feel as if I had never trained in the martial arts in my life, and have had me asking myself *"what the hell am I doing here?"* What I am doing is finding out my weak points and doing my best to understand and strengthen them.

If you train hard in any one system for many years you will reach a high standard, you may obtain a black belt and higher Dan grades. For anyone to get to that level means they have shown strength and commitment, but the biggest test comes from understanding that outside of that particular environment it means nothing.

Just as an example let's say your system is kickboxing. You have trained hard for many years and reached a high standard. Your punches are faster than lightning, and your roundhouse is faster than the rotors on a helicopter. But today you are fighting a yellow belt in a Judo club and by the rules of Judo. So no kicking and no punching, your years of training disappear and you are beaten by someone who may have only been training for six months. This does not mean that Judo is better than kick boxing or any other system, it shows you that by stepping out of the comfort of your own system, you are testing yourself and finding out your own weaknesses.

For me no one system has all the answers. If you want to train in only one system and you enjoy it then that's great. If you feel it covers all your needs and gives you what you want, then I wish you all the best and hope you enjoy your training for many years to come.

The Myths and Mistakes

Anything from being told what to do if someone grabs your lapel, or what to do if you are surrounded by a group of people.

Example: Person throws a punch, you are told to side kick them in the face then take the second and third person out with a hip throw and a hidden pressure point technique. IT WON'T HAPPEN.

Though ignorance or fear of being found out, many instructors will not bring real attitudes of street violence into their student's training. This also applies to the students because not all of them are willing to train with the reality needed to understand the real problem. Small class sizes don't pay bills. Remember anyone can make any thing work if their partner lets them do it. And pressure points disappear in a high-pressure confrontation or through thick clothing. Do you not think that in an, all-out no-holds barred fight, the fighter getting a beating would love to reach a pressure point and just by touching it have the 16 stone-monster rollover and have to be carried out of the ring? So mix your training if your karate instructor tells you that you can break away from a hold like this. Train with a Judo or Sambo instructor to feel how hard a grip can be, and before you can grab his wrist he will throw you on your back.

Finding what you want.

Today, all my training is looking for things that work within the brutal arena of the street, pub or tube station. For me, that's what I started training for. The enjoyment comes from training in all the fighting ranges, and improving the areas I am weakest in. I train to understand and deal with the type of attacker that is on the street today.

Your attacker today could just spray you in the face with CS Gas and stab you in the chest with a screwdriver, the attack is over before you realised it had begun. Say in the future the government decides that all citizens of the UK have the right to carry firearms (God forbid) then I would be the first to sign up for a course on how to use a Gun. So a large part of my training would have to change because my attacker's approach would be different with the introduction of firearms. I hope that the above never happens and it may sound a little extreme, but as I said before, my training is for self protection and I train to understand the attacker of today and not the attacker I may have had a hundred years ago.

You are the only person who can know why you train in the system you do, and the benefits you gain on a personal level are your own. But if the idea of protecting yourself on the street enters your head, you should not be complacent. Get out and add to what you have. You can still train and enjoy your base system and your Instructor should welcome this, if not then he knows that what he is teaching is weak.   If you have questions it's your right to have them answered. If you get attacked in the street, it's you who is on the spot, and only you who has to deal with it. Don't spend thousands of pounds on something you have doubts about be honest with yourself. If you went out and bought a new CD and found when you got home it did not play you would take it back and get a replacement. Because it was broken the shop would be willing to do so. But if you got home and found that your favourite artist was not up to scratch because they had changed their musical style then just because you don't like the new sound, doesn't mean you can take it back.

Let's go back for a second to the kick boxer and the Judo student, but this time the kick boxer and the judo man can only fight with kick boxing rules. What would be the outcome? Because the Judo man is no longer permitted to grab and throw, the kick boxer is going to feel a lot happier being in the environment he has trained for. I have lost count of the amount of times I have heard Instructors and students from many different systems talk about this and what would be the outcome. Events like the ultimate fight challenge and Vale Tudo championships have made many rethink their training in respect to what works under pressure. For me I think that it's a good thing and have the utmost respect for anyone who enters such events. But there are still rules.

What if one fighter had a knife, a broken bottle and steel toe-capped boots? Who would win? Lets go one step further, what if one fighter knew he could not handle the fight and stabbed his opponent before he could get into the ring. Am I going too far? Have I pushed my views beyond reality?
No this type of fighting goes on every day, and the worst part is that your attacker on the street will not enter the ring with music playing and lights flashing; you may not see him coming at all.

The window of opportunity

In a real situation you only have a small window of opportunity to attack first, and missing that moment will have you having to fight in the middle of a battlefield. So how can we start to build up pressure in our training and test what we have? I am not talking about ring craft here, but training to get you to understand the frantic and brutal 30 seconds of a real fight. But remember this is all without the real fear of being face to face with someone who could be about to kill you. How long? How far? How determined and how brutal can you be?

First kicking or punching.

Use what you hit hardest with and train it on a heavy bag until you are sick of it. Don't just have the bag hanging, lay it down on the floor and try your strikes now. Remember that in a real situation you need to hit hard and hit first.
If something goes wrong after that it comes down to your determination to win.
Use the bag as a partner hold the bag with one arm and strike with everything else, head, knees, elbows and biting. Start with 1min round's change your hold on the bag and start again, lay the bag on the floor and try it again. Restrict your movement by keeping a part of your body against the bag at all times. As you are striking the bag on the floor do not let that part of your body come off the bag. This is a hard and frustrating drill you will be tempted to come off the bag to drive in a hard technique, don't. Remember being uncomfortable is what you should be feeling. Build up your determination to fight on even when you feel sick to the stomach, and when to give up becomes harder to think about than not to keep going.

Cover and move in.

Moving forward once it's kicked off driving the fight into your attacker. I do not teach blocking, because it is something anyone will do if they see something coming at them. A 7 stone woman will not block and hold off a right hook from a 20 stone man. But if she moved in and grabbed him and shoved a nail file in his eye all bets are off. With a partner have them strike at your body with a pair of focus mitts, protect yourself by bending your arms and cover the side of your body. As the strikes are about to hit just move into the strike, do this drill in rounds of 4 strikes. That is, your partner attacks both sides of your body in turn. The pressure is taken on your arms not your ribs. Now build up the power in the strikes until your partner is hitting as hard as he or she can.

Now repeat the drill and this time as your partner attacks you move forward on the third or fourth blow. You will find you can say in control and even under heavy strikes be able to easily move in. Once you are in close your partner's strikes are not as effective. Plus the fact you have struck him in the balls and bitten his face off. The last two moves are up to you and how well you get on with your partner, but you will be amazed how quickly you can stop the attack just by moving in.

Keep your head down

We all feel it more with a bounce. Keep your chin down or close to your attacker if you are fighting close or on the floor. With a gap it's easier to move the head back or if struck the bounce given by the gap can knock you out. Open your mouth only if you are going to bite your attacker. Many people forget how dangerous the head can be when attacking, just because you have hold of his arms he can still do damage.

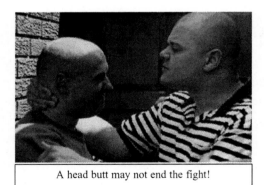

A head butt may not end the fight!

But when you're this close its something you can work with

And from a lot of angles

On the Ground

Ground fighting is something that has taken off big time with the success of the ultimate fight championships, and it is the range that brings me out in a cold sweat when I'm on the mat. But for the street it's the last place I would want to be. It's no good putting your attacker in pain with a leg lock, only to have his mate kick you in the face and his girlfriend stab you. But with a good training partner, working on the mat can take you to places other parts of your training cannot reach. I have found it the hardest, but also the most rewarding range. If you do any type of ground fighting I'm sure you would agree, if you have not done any ground fighting you are in for a great surprise.

To be good on the ground, the training and skill level you have to achieve is second to none. One drill my students enjoy. Is to get your partner to lay on his/her back. Then you lay face down across their chest, for 1minute your partner throws you off, you do not resist, but keep getting back on. The next part of the drill is the same as before but this time DON'T let your partner throw you off. No holding just spread your arms and legs and keep moving so he can't get you off. You will feel happier than someone who's just won the lottery but only when the drill is over.

Punched in the Face.

Having a good training partner and taking away the rules lets you test in the safety of the dojo (training hall) some of the real aspects of fighting on the street. Let's have a quick look at blocking and counter punching. With a partner let them throw punches and you block and counter. Now have your partner throw a punch hard and fast at your head, and a body punch that is so hard it will bring up the memory of last night's cheese on toast. At this point your block and counter may fall short of the mark. Because your partner is coming in hard, you are more likely to be grappling than counter punching.
It's great to work on technique. Finding the right way to throw a punch or kick is very important. The problem a lot of people have is too many techniques. When it comes to working under pressure they struggle because they are trying to decide which one to use. I feel a ground fighter is the best qualified to think about blocking because, if you practise blocking, you should also train in close combat and ground fighting. Because on the street there is a good chance that's where you will end up.

It's your choice.

As I said before having a base system is a good idea, and there is nothing wrong in wanting to add to it. Most systems work well within their own group, it's your choice if you want to step outside. The majority of Instructors who are interested in teaching self protection are open minded and only too willing to help you find the answers to your cross training needs. There is so much out there and we have the people here in the UK that can push you to your own limits.

You could check out Geoff Thompson's Animal Day training ideas. Train with Peter Consterdine and feel the power of the double hip strike. For how real it is on the streets get along to a seminar with Jamie O'Keefe. Have your eyes opened to practical knife defence that works with Peter Robins or Dave Turton for how brutal real fighting can be. Practise striking combinations with Kevin O'Hagan, Trevor Roberts for dealing with and being in the deep end of reality for years. For fear training do one training session with Darrin Richardson - handling your fear comes from training with him a second time.

Any one of the people above will help you find answers to the questions you may have about cross training. What you have to do is not look at a ring craft to help you with the problems of a real street a fight. And the best person to ask is the person who has been there and done it. It's your choice.

Chapter 17

Knifes, Bottles and Sharp Sticks

An insight to Knife Attacks

I'm sure that most people would believe having someone pull a knife on them is one of the most dangerous situations to be faced with. And in no way can I do justice to this subject in just one chapter which many take a lifetime to understand. I just want people to take away the flash ideas and deal with the deadly reality. Knife attacks seem to be getting more brutal and more attackers seem to cut or stab their victims even if the person has done what their attacker asked them to do. This leaves little room for doubt to just how dangerous someone with a knife is. Indeed any edged weapon should be treated with the greatest respect. The size of the blade does not matter, a 1-inch blade or a 7-inch blade or sharp pieces of wood have one thing in common; they can kill you. No matter how big and strong you are, you could have the muscle pumped body the size of a bus. But a small blade will easily cut away your flesh or puncture your lung.

A knife is deadly. I'm sure you're thinking that's as obvious as if you drop a stone it will hit the ground or giving a child a packet of crisps will be followed by the sounds of the vacuum cleaner. And you're right, but do you know what makes the knife more dangerous? It's the bollocks talked and given out by some people about how to deal with someone armed with a knife. It's bad enough when groups teach blocking or controlling wrist grabs without the reality of a strong non-compliant attack. The student is faced with trying to do something in the street that doesn't work. If lucky, they may just end up with a smack in the mouth and question why their training did not work. But if your attacker is armed, he may not only be willing to cut you, but you could be putting yourself in greater danger just by trying something unworkable.

We need to look closely at how knife attacks happen and who and what we should look out for. We have to get away from the standard view of knife attacks as a face off with the attacker lunging at you with the knife. Like many of you I have seen countless demos with knife attacks where the instructor controls the knife-attacking student, with controlled attacks and controlled defences. I mean would you like to grade in front of an Instructor who you made look like a Pratt the week before, because you attacked just a little bit too fast and his wonderful knife defence technique did not work?

Not only will you be taken off guard when faced with a real knife, but also the fear factor will take away most people's ability to anything about it. Add the fact that the chances of you actually seeing the knife that has stabbed or cut you are rare and it makes the idea of controlling a fast moving blade almost impossible. Like most things that work, simplicity is the key. You can do something to increase your chances of surviving a knife attack. The first step is to see and feel how quickly someone can cut and stab you in a frantic attack. With the truth being by the time you get control or get away you will have more holes in your body than a Tea Bag.

The Truth is in the Pen

As I said before in most cases of knife attacks the victim will not even see the knife (more about that later) but once the attack has begun it's a stabbing, slashing, frantic bloody mess. Before we go on I would like to get the point over to you in a real and safe way of just how big the problem of dealing with a frantic knife attack is. I would love to take credit for this training drill but the idea comes from my good friend Dave Turton 7th Dan Black Belt & Founder of the Self Defence Federation. This training drill will get the point across very quickly, and it will bring home the points I am trying to make within this chapter.

Face your partner, who is armed with a felt tipped pen, you will need to wear an old white tee shirt or shirt. Now get your partner to attack you with slashing and stabbing attacks. You both have to make it as real as possible. You have to make your partner want to make as many marks with the pen as they can. So add a financial incentive. As Dave Turton would say, *"The attacker gets half a crown for every pen mark on your shirt"*, for anyone reading this who was born after 1970 that's 25p. (A lot of money in Yorkshire) Within a short time you will find yourself covered in felt tip lines from the slashes and dots from the stabs. If you managed to grab your partner you will find marks all over your back, from your fingertips to your nose you will have more lines than an underground tube map. Take a good look at the marks and just think of the mess that you would be in if it had been a real knife or a broken beer glass. Still happy with your knife defences as you count up all the marks on your shirt? Or is a ray of doubt shining as you hand over the £5.00 you now owe your training partner?

What would you do?

If you don't know?

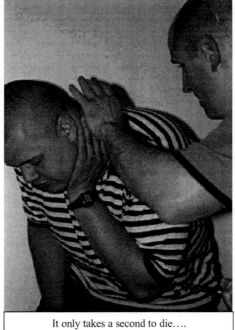

It only takes a second to die....

What is a Knife?

This may seem obvious, but the point is that you can use many things to cut and stab. So don't assume your attacker is going to have a six-inch blade with a wooden or plastic handle. If he shoved a sharp pencil into your throat it's just as deadly. Anything from a hand made hunting knife to a cheap craft knife. All are used on the streets, along with screwdrivers, bottles, beer glasses, pens, plastic and metal combs, the list goes on. Anything with a point or an edge is potentially dangerous, even your teeth could be classed as an edged weapon. You may agree, or have never thought of them in that way but it makes a good point that anything that can cut can do massive damage. If someone bites off your nose or your ear the effect is the same as if it had been cut with a blade, but it does seem more brutal.

Knives along with most stabbing or cutting weapons used on the street are easily obtained and easily replaced, and even without any special training anything with a point or edge is deadly. When I give seminars on knife defence I always make a point of demonstrating the cutting and stabbing power of items not normally thought of as weapons. People are taken back when they see how easily a credit card can cut though a large potato or the hard skin of a melon. So what is a knife? Almost anything that can cut or stab. Remember its not what type of weapon he has in his hand, it's what he is willing to do with it.

Unseen and Deadly

The real danger is the unseen attack that looks and feels like a punch but may have been a knife attack with all the deadly consequences coming from just one blow. Most martial arts have you trying to defend yourself against an attacker having the knife out in front of him slashing or lunging at you. Ok this can happen but if he is showing you the knife then he is someone who is more likely to be using it for intimidation purposes. So if you can see it flashing in front of you run away, keep it simple. He's showing you the knife to put the fear of God into you. A practical training idea would be drills in controlling your fear so you could run away. If you've got a gap use it, REMEMBER YOUR PEN COVERED SHIRT. How would you cope with an unseen attack? An attack made as you are fighting and rolling around the floor with your attacker then his best friend or girlfriend stabs you in the back when you are on the floor. There are many books, Videos and Instructors around teaching people how to defend themselves against a knife attack, but they tend to talk and show disarming techniques. Not many deal with the reality of how easy it is to be stabbed and how difficult it is to control.

Example, attacker moves in and stabs down at you with a knife. You cross your arms and block the attack, grab the attacking arm and lock with a twisting action to control, then put attacker into painful arm lock making the attacker drop the knife.

It's all well and good trying to give people confidence to deal with a situation if confronted by someone with a knife. But many of the things they talk about and expect you to do against a knife attack are bollocks. You can wrap the information up so many ways and say it will work in all these type of attacks and finish it off with a big red ribbon, but it's still bollocks. To talk about performing a complicated disarming technique is like juggling in quicksand, the more you move the deeper you sink. Practising something in a class or face to face with someone in the street are two different things. If it goes wrong in a class you can start again; if it goes wrong on the street the person with knife may be the last thing you ever see.

So how can we begin to control a deadly knife attack? The first step must be awareness of your surroundings and any confrontation must be viewed as a possible knife attack. Getting away from your attacker or destroying them before they have started their attack is the basic breakdown of knife defence. It is a sad fact that people who attack with a knife will attack when you cannot see the danger. From holding the knife behind their back or concealing it in their hand until its time for them to make their attack, everything is done to draw you into the trap.

You won't see the attack. Your only chance is to understand what is going on beforehand.

The attack can be from a powerful plunging thrust with their rear hand, as their left hand is in your face distracting you from the attack. You won't see it and it's to late to control. I hope you are feeling a little bit uncomfortable in your seat at this moment. If you just think about that and the consequences for a moment are you feeling just a little bit sick?

Seeing the Unseen

Not only is the speed that someone can cut their victim terrifying but just thinking about why someone is willing to cut and stab a helpless victim will drive you crazy. You could sit around a table and discuss the rights and wrong for years and never get the answer to why. But the one thing you have to get clear from the outset with regard to people using knifes is that people do.

Your assessment of any situation you may find yourself in is the key to not being a victim. Not only someone punching you but also someone stabbing you, they both start with the same threat. Threat assessment is something you can assess over time from the number of people around you to the place and time. And if you feel that you are in a dangerous situation you should always act on that feeling and get away. But let's look at what you can do if you find yourself confronted and the only option you have left is a physical one. It's the same as if it was a fistfight and that is you being pre-emptive with your physical response to the threat of an attack. Your attacker can give off some physical signs that they have a knife but you may not see them. (You should always assume that your attacker is armed.)

Your attacker's confidence comes from the knife and they will always make sure it is to hand. From keeping one hand out of sight or the way they hold their arm straight with their fingertips curled up out of sight, or a hand tucked into their jacket or rubbing their hands on the outside of their pocket just making sure the knife is there. These are just some of the signals given off by someone who is armed and wants to take you off guard. But the fact that you are being confronted can make these signals difficult to see if you are not prepared to think that anyone could be carrying a knife. If you only practise knife defence in respect to someone already having the knife out in front of them. Then you will miss the signs and will not be prepared for what happens next.

From a group of people standing around you, the person who stabs you could run from behind the group, he pushes them aside and plunges a knife in you. Just think, a small wound to your body can have your internal body pressure start to force your intestines out of your body. All this and when you fall to the floor the rest of the group can kick what's left all over the pavement.

In the same way you develop speed and power in your punch or kick it takes time and practise. So add to your training some hidden knife attacks, just to practise looking for the signals someone concealing a knife gives off. With a training partner stand close to each other one of you hold a knife and try and conceal it from your training partner. Please don't use a real blade. Now try and pull out the knife not to attack but just to get the knife ready for an attack. You are training not to see the knife but to recognise body language, look for unnatural movements of hands, arms and legs. Check how many times you can't see their hands or their fingertips, remember the only warning you may have is someone just putting their hand into a pocket. From just a simple movement they can pull a knife and attack before you can react.

If you control the attacker before the knife is pulled you have a better chance of getting away from the situation or controlling the vital few seconds you have before the attack. You could tell them to show you their hands and if they refuse you could attack straight away. Or maybe better still, make your body language less aggressive. You could bring one of your hand's in line with the attacker's arm that you feel is reaching for a knife. This will help if you do not attack in time because if your attacker pulls the knife your arm is already covering the angle of attack.

Be First

If you feel threatened this is the time you should act. Don't wait for the knife to come out to make sure; you are wasting time, go with your feelings. Your hands should be forward in the fence position, move you're leading hand to cover the suspect arm. Now attack with your best technique. Hit hard and finish off. Let me make it clear, if you feel that you are in danger, then to delay could result in you being stabbed. Be first. We are talking about a violent confrontation, not your mum asking if you would like a cup of tea. If the knife is pulled and does not cut you the first time you are in a stand off and in greater danger. I have been involved in 5 situations where the person had a knife and only in one of these did I see the knife before hand. The other times the blade was found afterwards or seen by someone I was working with. God knows how many people I have been in contact with who have had something hidden. Give no one the benefit of the doubt, treat any confrontation as armed.

Cover the problem

Jamming and covering techniques work well. With jamming techniques you are controlling the arm you suspect the attacker is holding a weapon in. This could be with your lead hand touching the attacker's arm or keep your hand just away from the attacker's arm keeping a relaxed open handed gesture. Again as soon as you feel in danger from them moving forward or a hand moving out of sight, cover their arm and attack.

Let's look at a couple of drills that bring home the point. If you stand in front of a partner get them to point a finger at your throat and then rest it on your Adams apple. Now when they like they can push you in the throat just hard enough to make you move back and cough. You have to try and push their hand away as soon as they start to push. You will find yourself coughing more times than Kurt Russell in the film Back Draft. Now do the same thing again but this time your partner cannot push you in the throat until they see you move to push their hand away. You will find this much more comfortable, I have seen this trick put forward as some fantastic skill level of an Instructor. It's not action will beat reaction.

Let's go back to the felt tip again. Have your partner hold the pen behind his back and face each other. Now have him attack you with stabbing or slashing attacks, but only one attack at a time. You can only move out of the away when you see him move to attack. Looks like another trip to the laundrette for your old white shirt. Now do the same again but this time he cannot attack you with the pen until he sees you move. So line up your partner with a good right hook with more firepower than a small army. Remember he can't move, until you make your attack so let him have it right on the jaw and see his unconscious body hit the deck. ONLY JOKING but it made the point. Always treat someone as armed and if you feel you are about to be attacked and you have no other option BE FIRST.

The person who is willing to use a knife in a fight may be soft and weak without a knife, but cold and deadly with it. They will stab you from your blind side, or when you are beaten to the floor will carry on the attack, cutting and stabbing as you lay helpless on the ground. The people who do this cannot be bargained with; it is hard to bargain with someone who has just opened the side of your face with a razor. Telling him that this is not a civilised way of carrying on in a democratic society, believe me will be falling on deaf ears. Remember someone with a knife in his or her hand is holding death.

I have been lucky enough to train with some great Instructors in regard to knife defence. I'm sure you will understand that I cannot do justice to all that there is to know about knife defence in just one chapter in one book. So let's waste no more time and look at the first rule if someone has pulled a knife on you. This rule will work in the majority of situations apart from maybe a telephone box.

And any good knife defence Instructor will call it the first rule. If someone confronts you and they pull out a knife and you can see it, Run Like a Bastard. It is simple and easy to remember. I'm not joking. If you can run why not? Is it your macho ego that is telling you to stay and have a battle with this knife wielding maniac or because you feel you have to do something physical to win? If you run away and wake up the next morning you've won. You may be thinking *"what if I can't run?"* Point taken. But lets get this first rule across, I personally have the type of figure a company could design a new type of whaling ship on. But if someone pulls a knife on me, I will run and accelerate away quicker than a Porsche.

People who use knifes, bottles or even a sharp stick, do so because they feel they have the weaker hand if forced to fight, they need all the help they can get. This is not a justification for stabbing someone just because you like the look of his watch. I'm saying that if you pick up a knife or any weapon, you are doing so because you don't like the odds and the sight of a knife will make a weak person appear a giant. If the attack is for money the person with the knife many show the knife openly, or tell you they have one.

This is a terrifying situation and you are very likely to freeze to the spot. This is the effect the attacker wants, you are weak and he feels powerful and in control. Adrenalin and all its affects get to work, your increased heart rate, tunnel vision, shaking and sweating does all the work for him. He can now move in and with luck just take your money, car keys or anything that he likes the look of. After taking your money you are left in a state of shock, for a long time afterwards you will feel bad and angry about what happened. You will play over and over the encounter many times in your head,

"Could I have done something, could I have fought back? Why did he have to take my wedding ring? I should have told him to go fuck himself and dropped kicked him in the face".

We can all daydream about what we would like to do when faced with an attacker. Dreams can sometimes feel better than the reality of our real lives, but to daydream about what you would do against a knife attack is deadly.

What you have to do is face the fact that it happened. You survived the encounter without getting killed or having your face cut to pieces. Don't condemn yourself for being scared, learn from it and move on. It could have been a lot worse. Say your attacker was much more aggressive. You could have been walking along a street when he walked up to you asking the time. As you look at your watch he opens the side of your face with a razor or pushes a screwdriver into your chest, you could now be dying on the pavement. This happens on the street, no discussion just out of the blue and brutal.

Covering the Ground

If you are face to face with someone who is threatening you with a knife you are in a very dangerous situation, but if you can see it, you have a chance. Look at it this way, if someone wanted to cut you they would just do it. Many victims of knife attacks do not know that they have even been stabbed or cut. Because they did not see that the person had a knife they assumed they had just been punched. In fact the realisation that you have been stabbed is more likely to come some time after the attack.

The distance between you and the knife is where we can start looking at what to do to take control of a knife threat. But I'm going to say this one more time: if the person with the knife is not close and you're not in a telephone box RUN. It is very unlikely your attacker will come after you once you have started your own personal land speed record. As I said before the person carrying the knife does so because it makes him or her feel stronger and more confident. If we look at a knife attack as a stand off the last thing in the world they are going to expect is you attacking them.

You have to cover the ground in front of you and take the fight to them. You have to close the attack down. The knife itself is not the enemy, the person holding the blade is. Make the attacker unconscious and the knife becomes no more dangerous than a banana. (Sorry to any banana systems out there) The point I am trying to make is that jamming the attacking arm and striking hard to the face, or grabbing the attacker's arms then head butting him in the face before he makes his attack is practical.

You must stop the attack, take them out. Push his eye ball so hard that it feels it will hit the back of his brain, grab his throat and pull so hard it's no longer part of his body. Some of you may be thinking that's a bit over the top, how come this person is about to cut you? We are talking about a situation that has developed into an all out nightmare. The threat of a situation should have been dealt with before the person had time to pull out the knife by hitting first when you were confronted or better still getting away when you first felt the situation developing. If your back is against the wall you have to become your attacker's nightmare, taking their comfort blanket of having a knife away by attacking them.

Attack hard, attacking their eyes, throat or groin. Your control on the situation is to take them out. Anything less is dangerous.

From the Movies

Before I say any more I would like to cover this point. There is no different happy answer I can give you to dealing with every possible knife attack, or situation a knife attack can develop from. I was once asked at a seminar, *"what do I do if I wake up in my bed with someone sitting on top of me and holding a knife to my throat"? "Any Bloody thing he tells you to do"*, was my reply. It was not the answer she wanted to hear. She had taken her personal fear of being attacked to her ultimate nightmare. All you had to do was have the attack take place in a hotel room by a man called Norman whose mother didn't say much, and it would have been the scene from a movie. Yes it can happen, so can you winning the lottery. But you are more likely to be faced with a situation in the street or a domestic situation that has got way out of control. You should understand that if you are protecting yourself in a situation with a knife you are going to get cut. If you wake up with a knife to your throat you are in deep shit. But if your attacker is making demands you still have a fighting chance. It comes down to picking the right time, do or say anything that can give you a fighting chance. Or better still make sure your doors and windows are locked before you go to bed.

Do Anything to Survive

Let's put it this way, say you are asleep in bed one night and you wake up in the early hours of the morning desperate for a drink of water. So you make your way down stairs to the kitchen. As you stand there in the early morning light drinking the cold water, you hear someone run out of the darkness and up the stairs behind you. What would you do? All the hairs on the back of your neck stand up. You know that you are the only one up, the kids are asleep upstairs. On the kitchen table is the family bread knife. Would you pick it up? Would it make you feel happier to deal with the monster that has just run up your stairs? Suddenly you hear one of your children screaming. You grab the knife and run up the stairs, the bread knife in your hand is your equaliser. You say to yourself, *"If that monster's attacking my children he's going to have to have a gun to stop me"*

Anyone of us would help a loved one, we would not worry about having or needing a knife. The above story is made up to get you to understand that we can all, if fighting for the right reasons, do anything to survive. If anyone is willing to use a knife to attack you then they have no right to expect anything less than if the fight is hand-to-hand and anything goes. You should feel that if I die in defending a loved one or myself, before they do the post-mortem on my body they will have to remove my attacker's testicles from my left hand and his eyeball from my right hand. I never want to be in that position.

But if I am, I need to train with the right attitude and with techniques that will work under the intense pressure I will face within a knife attack.

Covering and Attacking

A trained knife fighter will lead with one hand and stab with the rear. With the lead hand distracting you from the attack the rear hand holding the knife plunges quickly and repeatedly into your body.

The following drills will get you working very close to your partner. You can use them for attacking as someone is reaching for a knife or if the knife is out and the attack has started. The hard part is getting to grips with the idea of moving in and closing down the attack. Also you can add to any of the drills throwing something at the attacker. For training purposes you could use a focus mitt, plastic cup or a boxing glove, to simulate throwing an ashtray or a hand full of coins at your attacker. The idea being, if what you throw hits and causes damage to you attacker, great. At least you will get a reaction that can give you an extra second to move in. Also add dialogue; don't train as if you're in a silent movie. By shouting something out of context to distract them or by being passive and talking softly to distract them before you attack.

But dealing with a lead hand attack to the face and rear handed knife attack, your options are limited. Your instinct is to react to the hand in your face first and the reality is that you will be too late to protect your body. See the whole picture and in training try and override the lead hand attack, see the danger of the rear hand.

Inside-outside hard and soft

The drills can be looked at in two ways. First inside means you are moving inside the attacking arm and face to face with the attacker. Outside means you are outside the attacking arm or have jammed the attacker's arm across their body. Also train the lead hand and rear attack dealing with the lead hand quickly and moving in on the outside of your attacker. The idea with the drills is to make the attacks as real as possible.

Remember this is your last chance because you should have taken the person out before they started the attack.

For safety in training use rubber knifes or felt tipped pens. Training soft means the attack is still determined, but your strikes to the target area are controlled but not pulled back. Always strike through the target. Training hard means the attacks are fast and determined with the defender moving in and striking as hard as they can, BUT striking the attacker's chest or shoulder, for safety. Your real target areas being their eyes, throat and groin.

1st Drill

Face your partner, Your partner is going to attack with a rear knife attack. With your lead hand covering the angle of attack. Move in jamming your lead hand and forearm against the attacking arm. Strike hard to the face, throat, eyes or groin. Keep striking until the threat is over, driving forward all the time. When I say groin I mean your attacker's, don't start arm locking and moving the direction of the weapon, that's another type of bollocks. Don't try and grab the knife hand, jam and cover the attacking arm between their wrist and elbow. The attacker can stab or slash to the leg, groin, body, chest or face. You will find that the quicker you move in the less you have to think about where the knife attack is going. Control the bigger target: the arm holding the knife not the smaller fast moving wrist.

2nd Drill

Face your partner; your partner attacks with the knife coming from across their body. Simulating someone pulling a knife from inside their jacket or having concealed the knife by folding their arms. Your lead hand jams and pushes the attacker's forearm into their body as you make your attack. If your partner is side on jam, the attacking arm between the shoulder and elbow turning their back to you.

3rd Drill

Work with drills 1 and 2; but this time the person with the knife attacks with his lead hand first. By pushing his hand into your face this will distract you from the blade in his rear hand. It's hard to ignore the hand in your face, but your attention must be on the blade.

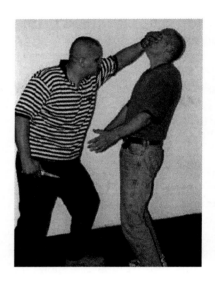 

Covering techniques can also be used if the attacker moves away then comes in from say 2 or 3 feet. Your leading or rear hand moves across your body, as you move to the inside or outside of the attack. You do not move back from the attack, you move in. You will find out quickly that it's not a different technique for each attack but confidence in just one or two ideas that work under pressure. All knife attacks to head, body or legs all start at the same point the first movement of the attackers arm. Ideally make the attacker unconscious before he gets his hands on the knife, failing that close it down give them no room to move and inflict as much damage as possible. Don't try and perform a 22-piece take down doing your best Jackie Chan or Claude Van Damme impression. I am sorry to say that it doesn't work that way. Leave that fantasy where it is enjoyable and belongs on the big screen.

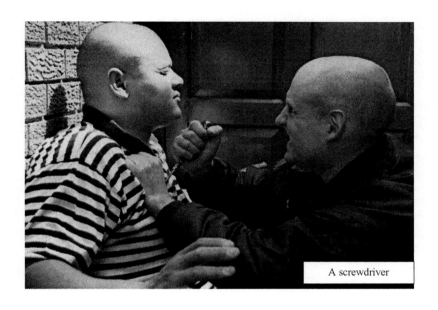

A screwdriver

A hammer

A brick

It doesn't have to be sharp to kill you!

Awareness must be the most important part of training for knife defence. So you should practise how to spot someone who could be about to attack. Practise closing down your partner before they have made their attack. Use anything around to help, if you have time and you see the threat from a distance. If I could, I would throw, house bricks, bottles, tables, anything that came to hand. Do anything you can before you end up in a knife stand off. You will soon find in the training drill that the longer you wait the more you get stabbed, so please when practising only use rubber knives. Anything you are carrying can be replaced, you cannot. This must be your first thought if confronted. Do everything you can to avoid getting involved but if you are in fear of your personal safety and the threat of an attack in imminent DON'T WAIT. Survive first, deal with the outcome later; defend yourself in court afterwards, if you have to. Unfortunately muggers and their ilk don't wear labels so any approaching individual unknown to you is a potential armed attacker. This may sound a little bleak but it's just the way it is.

A personal view

I hope you have found this book helpful no matter what your background. Throughout I have tried to be as honest as I can in my views. Some of you may have found some of them as popular as Gary Glitter doing a come back tour. But if this book has given you a talking point or given you a few ideas that you would like to add to your training, then it has done its job.

Only your willingness to see how real a situation can get can prepare you and make you able to handle it. You can justify anything to yourself if you are not willing to step outside your training. Confidence to handle a situation can only come from facing up to it in your training. How else will you know what you can do?

Walk away if you can it is the best option. If you can't, you have to take the offensive and attack first.

How do you get the confidence to walk away and not have the feeling of being weak? How do you get the better of your ego so you can just walk away? If your training puts you under pressure and tests the full range of your fighting ability then you can build confidence in yourself. As you get more confident in one area move out of that comfort zone and try a new one. It is not easy, but that's the whole point, you are building confidence. You cannot build a floor at a time, but brick by brick.

We are lucky to have so many ways to get information about any type of training, from books, videos, magazines, seminars and instructors. Always check systems out, ask for information what do they cover? Go along and see a class. It takes time but its better to get the best rather than staying with something that teaches crap, just because its an easy class and only five minutes walk from your home. It's your choice.

You should always enjoy your training. But if it does not push you, you are not building a stronger house just patching up the old one. OK, you have a comfortable chair and TV but the roof is leaking and one day you may be hit by a tornado.

Thanks again for taking the time to read Awareness Fears and Consequences and I hope you achieve all the goals you set yourself. Remember it's your right to protect yourself, only you are responsible and only you can do anything about it.

Best Wishes

Alan Charlton June 2001

The End

PREVENT YOURSELF FROM BECOMING A VICTIM
'Dogs don't know Kung Fu'
A guide to Female Self Protection
By Jamie O'Keefe £14 including post & packing
Never before has Female Self Protection used this innovative approach to pose questions like. Why do Rapist's Rape? Why are Women abused? Why do Stalkers Stalk? This book takes a look at all Simple, Serious, and Life threatening aspects of Self Protection that concern us daily, along with **PREVENTION** of Child abuse and Child Abduction, Emotional cruelty, Telephone abuse, Road rage, Muggers, Date rape, Weapon attacks, Female abduction, Sexual Assault & Rape, Self defence law, and what it will allow us to do to protect ourselves, plus much more. With over 46,500 words, 77 pictures and 200 printed pages 'Dog's Don't Know Kung fu' is a no nonsense approach to women's self defence. It covers many realistic scenarios involving Children's abduction as well as typical attacks on women. Besides quoting actual events, the book explains how to avoid trouble and how you should react if you get into a situation.
__This book is a 'must read' for all women and parents.__
It is also important for teenage women, but, due to some of its graphic depiction's of certain incidences, parents should read it first and decide if it's suitable for their child.

www.newbreedbooks.co.uk

What makes tough guys tough?

The Secret Domain

WHAT MAKES

TOUGH GUYS
TOUGH
The Secret Domain
by Jamie O'Keefe

Written by Jamie O'Keefe

Jamie O'Keefe has interviewed key figures from boxing, martial arts, self-protection, bodyguards, doorwork, military, streetfighting and so on. Asking questions that others were too polite to ask but secretly wanted to know the answers.

Interviews include **Peter Consterdine, Geoff Thompson,** and **Dave Turton** from the countries leading self-protection organisations 'The British Combat Association' and the 'Self Defence Federation.' Along with Boxing heroes **Dave 'Boy' Green** and East London's former Commonwealth Champion **'Mo Hussein.' Plus unsung heroes from the world of Bouncers, Foreign Legion, Streetfighters, and more.**

This book also exposes the Secret Domain, which answers the question 'What makes tough guys tough.'

Find out what some of the toughest guys on the planet have to say about 'What makes tough guys tough' and how they would turn you into a tough guy.

Available from NEW BREED at £14 inc p&p

www.newbreedbooks.co.uk

Pre-emptive strikes
for winning fights
'The alternative to grappling'

by
Jamie O'Keefe
£14 inc P&P
from
New Breed
Po Box 511
Dagenham, Essex RM9 5DN

www.newbreedbooks.co.uk

THUGS, MUGS
and
VIOLENCE

REVIEWED AS
'BOOK OF THE MONTH'
Front magazine

£14 inc p&p
from
NEW BREED
Po box 511, Dagenham Essex RM9 5DN

www.newbreedbooks.co.uk

AVAILABLE NOW

BY
Kevin O'Hagan
£14 inc Post and packing
from
New Breed, Po box 511
Dagenham, Essex RM9 5DN

The latest book by Jamie O'Keefe

In Your Face
'CLOSE QUARTER FIGHTING'
by
Kevin O'Hagan

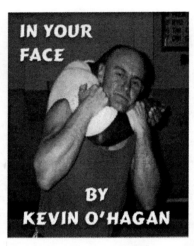

£14 each from NEW BREED

I THOUGHT
You'd be
BIGGER !

A SMALL PERSONS
guide to
FIGHTING BACK
by Kevin O'Hagan